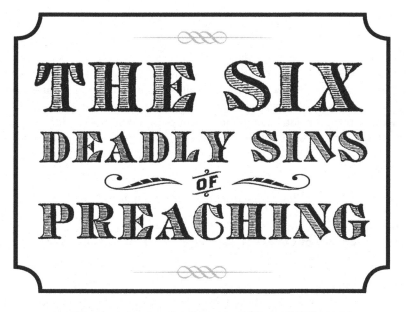

THE SIX DEADLY SINS OF PREACHING

BECOMING RESPONSIBLE FOR THE FAITH WE PROCLAIM

ROBERT STEPHEN REID AND LUCY LIND HOGAN

ABINGDON PRESS
Nashville

THE SIX DEADLY SINS OF PREACHING
BECOMING RESPONSIBLE FOR THE FAITH WE PROCLAIM

This book is printed on acid-free paper.

Library of Congress Cataloging-in-Publication Data

Reid, Robert Stephen.
  The six deadly sins of preaching : becoming responsible for the faith we proclaim / Robert Reid and Lucy Lind Hogan.
      p. cm.
   ISBN 978-1-4267-3539-4 (book - pbk. / trade pbk. : alk. paper) 1. Preaching. 2. Christian ethics. I. Hogan, Lucy Lind, 1951– II. Title.
   BV4235.E75R45 2012
   251—dc23

                                                                        2012007062

12 13 14 15 16 17 18 19 20 21—10 9 8 7 6 5 4 3 2 1

MANUFACTURED IN THE UNITED STATES OF AMERICA

CONTENTS

Acknowledgments v

1: Irresponsible Preaching 1
    Needed: A Practical Ethics of Preaching
    Six Deadly Sins? I Thought There Were Seven!
    A Typology of Irresponsible Preaching
    Missteps, Unthinking Mistakes, and the Call to Virtue

2: The Pretender 17
    The Pretender and the Problem of In-Authenticity
    The Virtue of Authenticity

3: The Egoist 29
    The Egoist and the Problem of Self-Absorption
    The Virtue of Humility

4: The Manipulator 41
    The Manipulator and the Problem of Greediness
    The Virtue of Carefulness

5: The Panderer. 53
    The Panderer and the Problem of Trendiness
    The Virtue of Honesty

6: The Demagogue 67
    The Demagogue and the Problem of Exploitation
    The Virtue of Woo

Contents

7: The Despot 79
    The Despot and the Problem of Self-Righteousness
    The Virtue of Being a "Namer of God"

8: Wait! Wait! There's More! 93
    An Abecedarium of Missteps
    More Missteps or Lapses in Judgment

Epilogue: Becoming Responsible for the Faith We Proclaim 105
    A Tale of Two Preachers
    The Greatest of These . . .

A Code of Ethics for Preachers 111

Notes 115

ACKNOWLEDGMENTS

Robert Stephen Reid thanks the members of the Academy of Homiletics who have taught him more than they know about preaching through conversation, practice, and writings; the preachers of his acquaintance who struggle with more than a few of these temptations while aspiring to live into these virtues; and the University of Dubuque for its continued professional support of his inquiry into how religious communication, in all of its forms, functions to call forth faith from listeners.

Lucy Lind Hogan is most grateful to Kevin, Susan, and Bruce, who have served as wonderful sounding boards and helped keep her preaching on the faithful path. Likewise, she would like to thank all of the students and preachers who offered stories and examples of preachers they have known and loved, and those who served as examples of what not to do. She would like to thank Wesley Theological Seminary for graciously granting a sabbatical year in which to work on this project. And finally, she would like to thank Bob, who is a great writing partner.

Chapter One

IRRESPONSIBLE
🖎 PREACHING ∞

What Bob remembers the most is the moment during his sermon on the evils of gambling when the preacher stepped over the line. The preacher was earnest and clearly well meaning. He clutched his Bible as he spoke, as if its visible presence substantiated the truths of his lesson. The moment occurred while he was deep into describing how the sin of gambling is one of the principal ways the devil takes hold of the soul of a man to devour him.

Gambling parlors, we were told, were dens of iniquity to be avoided at all costs. A young person then, Bob had no idea where he might go to gamble, let alone why it would be a parlor. Slot machines, roulette wheels, cards, and the other paraphernalia of gambling were lifted up one by one in the sermon and properly vilified as the means of traducing men away from their godly commitment to provide for their families.

Then came the moment when the preacher singled out the evils of dice.

Something about dice clearly transfixed this man. Dice were not just used for immoral purposes; they were "evil in and of themselves." To hold dice in your hands was to actually be in the grip of evil.

Brash teenager that he was when he heard this sermon, Bob waited for the greeting line to thin out. With his friends watching and with all the impertinence of youth, he shook the pastor's hand and asked, "Pastor, if dice are evil in and of themselves, is it evil to play Monopoly?"

The pastor paled; he loved to play Monopoly with his family. Yet, the implications of the sermonic claim had been challenged. What most people present had experienced as simple, down-home, country-style preaching, carried away in naming and warning parishioners to avoid the temptations of sin, had been called out. In his effort to underscore his point about temptation, the pastor had engaged in the preacherly practice of overreaching to make a point. It was hardly irresponsible behavior. But right there, in the greeting line, is where the true sermonic misstep occurred.

"I'll never play Monopoly again."

1

It was as if Bob had caught him in an unknowing sin. Having become aware of it, his only option was to forswear now and forever any recourse to its seductions. That was the moment the preacher stepped through the looking glass. Both he and Bob knew there was nothing wrong with Monopoly dice. But rather than back off of a simple sermonic embellishment, rather than risk appearing to be an unreliable interpreter of God's word, he dogmatically reified his claim: all dice are evil. He had been pushed to a pastoral precipice and chose to step off the edge rather than allow his reliability as a faithful interpreter of God's truth to be placed in peril.

Of course, the irony is whatever faith Bob and the other watching teenagers had placed in their preacher's interpretive office was dispelled that day. His unwillingness to back off of a patently absurd claim made him appear unreliable in their eyes.

Bob's story is hardly an isolated instance of watching a preacher misstep. Some cases are more egregious than others, but there is no end to the stories that can be told of preachers who misstep and misspeak in matters of faith. Lucy and Bob would be the first to admit that in their thirty years of preaching each of them can recall many occasions when they realized, in hindsight, that they stepped over a line. So when does a misstep become irresponsible?

Most parishioners are more forgiving than brash teenagers. They overlook the occasional missteps on the part of their pastor who has demonstrated his or her care in so many other ways. Just as in friendships and marriage, missteps on the part of one person in a relationship are instances of normal human failings and idiosyncrasies. We all experience these regularly, forgive them, forget them, or simply see them as minor and sometimes even endearing flaws in the people we love. But when missteps become a pattern that gains prominence in a person's behavior, they often lead to irresponsible practice. In the pulpit this tendency can lead to what we call irresponsible preaching—a situation in which our trust in the minister should be called into question.

More than any other issue, the question of plagiarizing sermons has made preachers acutely aware of how the misstep of namelessly borrowing sermon material can turn from a time-crunch temptation into a pattern of practice. And although Bob was simply amused at his pastor's misstep, a colleague of Lucy was far from amused when she discovered that her pastor was preaching other people's sermons without attribution. That pastor had arrived as a highly respected preacher to occupy a premier pulpit in Washington, DC. Yet, soon after his arrival she realized he was preaching sermons downloaded from the Internet. Lucy's friend felt betrayed. How could she trust anything her pastor said or did once she realized his preaching ministry was pretense?

Homileticians Joseph Jeter and Anna Carter Florence claim that regular borrowing and outright stealing from the extraordinary amount of resources available to preachers on the Internet can become an addiction.[1] What begins as research thoughtfully engaging a biblical text can easily become a time-saving choice simply to copy and paste someone else's witness to faith and then present it as one's own. It's a problem because it's not just the words that are borrowed; it's the witness that is borrowed as well. Good sermons arise as part of the preacher's dialogue with Scripture, self, potential listeners, experience, a theological tradition, the culture's questions, and with the reflections other preachers have tendered on the subject. When it stops being a dialogue, then it stops being a sermon. It becomes a reading of someone else's sermon or a pastiche of sermonic reflections by others. In the end it is an issue of trustworthiness. Is the preacher giving witness to his or her own faith or the faith of another? Can the congregation trust that what the preacher proclaims is honestly his or her own convictions about God and faith? We will return to a discussion of this vice in the next chapter.

Plagiarism is simply one of a number of bad habits preachers can fall into as a practice. Most preachers would be chagrined to discover that people—even their own parishioners—might view some of their pulpit practices as unethical. Formal ministerial codes of ethics as formulated by denominations rarely if ever venture into the waters of identifying responsible and irresponsible pulpit conduct. And when the subject of ethics is raised in seminary homiletics courses it typically is treated as a theological concern of preaching rather than as an expressive function of its practice.[2] Textbooks on practical ministerial ethics are more apt to discuss responsible and irresponsible behaviors in the pulpit. Yet even here most of this advice is reserved for the interpersonal activities of pastoral ministry rather than for the homiletical practice itself. And when they do take up the subject it tends to be occasional (what comes to the minds of the writers) rather than something grounded in a particular approach to ethical practice.[3] What appears to be largely absent in current literature on preaching is a practical book that identifies a continuum of the virtues and vices of pulpit practice.[4]

 ## NEEDED: A PRACTICAL ETHICS OF PREACHING

Most preachers do not set out to misspeak or to preach irresponsibly. It is the rare preacher who graduates from seminary thinking, "From now on I won't ever have to write another paper or sermon again. I'll just download my sermons from the Internet."

Nevertheless, irresponsible preaching represents an ethical failure by the minister. In part it occurs when the braking system that should keep such failures from occurring is somehow ineffective or absent. It also occurs when preachers fail to either identify or at least truly make their own some criterion of responsible pulpit practice. These need to be practices that both honor God and honor the preacher's listeners.

3

In this book we invite you to identify and reflect on both the virtues and vices that preachers do well to observe. Our goal is modest. Though it certainly participates in the genre of ethical reflection, this book is not intended to serve as a fully developed ethics of preaching. Rather, we offer it to readers as a contribution to virtue ethics literature. As such, we begin by grounding our notion of Christian ethics in the character of the preacher. Historically ethics has tried to arrive at a descriptive notion of the good and derive from it pre-scriptive notions about moral oughts. But contemporary philosophical ethics is fraught with problems in trying to arrive at the criterion for all this. The ques-tion always boils down to whose good and which oughts? In this volume, we do not assume that there are commonly accepted grounds for determining what ethics is (its description) or what it is for (its prescriptions). For this reason we take the approach that a practical ethics of preaching should be grounded in the character of the individual and in a tradition of virtues that support practices characterized by integrity.

An illustration may help here. One cannot determine whether an action should take place without first considering whom the person is who is taking the action. Most of us believe it is wrong for a person to fire a weapon at an-other individual for the purpose of maiming or even killing that person. We can, however, imagine that this action could be responsible and appropriate for an officer of the law. But even when an officer-involved shooting occurs, we be-lieve that the character of that officer should be examined. Has this officer been involved in too many such shootings? Did the situation justify excessive force? The character of the individual and how a community understands the action that took place are all involved in determining whether the practice should be considered a responsible or an irresponsible exercise of force. The fact that we believe the character of the officer involved in the shooting should be examined is a way of admitting that, drastic as the situation that called forth the action may have been, it can still be considered virtuous. Acceptance of what otherwise would be a terrible action functionally supports a notion of civility in our com-mon commitment to living together in community.

If we apply the same consideration to the practice of preaching, character is always at the center of ethical conduct and clergy should speak and act virtuous-ly in the pulpit because not to do so, over time, is to model a vision of character incapable of sustaining what it means to participate in a *communio sanctorum.* This is Calvin's phrase for the community of saints divinely chosen to fulfill their vocation in glorifying God's name. When a preacher borrows material and presents it as his or her own, or regularly chooses to pander to the trendy interests of listeners rather than to present the gospel, that preacher shapes the character of what counts as faith and faithfulness for the congregation, whether he or she is aware of the pretense or not.

What matters from this viewpoint is not the fateful decision to engage in some unethical or less-than-responsible activity. In our experience preachers rarely face the yawning chasm of a do-or-die ethical choice in preaching. Rather, irresponsible preaching happens because a minister discovers that unthinking mistakes did not raise any dust. Going down this pathway, what we term a misstep may actually be quite well received by a congregation. What started as a misstep eventually becomes justified as the preacher's acceptable norm of practice, and the seed of irresponsible preaching is born. It is the sum of steps that create a practice, whether for good or ill. However, when individuals rely on the integrity of making responsible choices in preaching, they contribute to forming the *communio sanctorum.*

Our commitment to this belief leads us to affirm that a responsible ethics of preaching is embodied in both how choices are made and in the character of the one who makes the choices. Where traditional ethics often focus on the anticipated end products of actions, this conception of ethics assumes that the issue of who is doing the preaching and the choices he or she is making is what matters formatively for the faith of the community and for that person's own faith formation.[5] Our approach participates in the tradition of ethical reflection on virtues as a way of looking at how consistent moral behavior, seen or unseen, sustains an ethic of homiletic faithfulness to God and reliability for listeners.

SIX DEADLY SINS?
I THOUGHT THERE WERE SEVEN!

We all love lists. Turn to *USA Today* or any number of websites and you will find lists of everything imaginable, from the best and worst places to live to the ten fruits and vegetables guaranteed to melt away the pounds. This love of lists is nothing new. Moses traveled up the mount to meet God and returned with what? A list. In Proverbs we are told that:

> There are six things that the LORD hates,
> seven that are an abomination . . .
> haughty eyes, a lying tongue,
> and hands that shed innocent blood,
> a heart that devises wicked plans,
> feet that hurry to run to evil,
> a lying witness who testifies falsely,
> and one who sows discord in a family. (Prov. 6:16-19)

Paul loved lists, too. His letters are filled with them: gifts of the Spirit (1 Cor. 12:4-11), fruits of the Spirit (Gal. 5:22-23), the various members of the body (1 Cor. 12:27-30), and the dreaded works of the flesh—sorcery, quarrelling, and carousing, to name only three of fifteen (Gal. 5:19-21).

For years, Lucy has invited students in her introductory preaching class to write reflections on the preachers they want to be like and preachers they do

not want to emulate. Then she asks them to identify the qualities, the characteristics, and the virtues and vices of these preachers. Their reflections stimulate
a lively discussion and fascinating lists of "Good Preaching/Preachers" on one
side of a blackboard and "Not-Good Preaching/Preachers" on the other. What
surprises Lucy each year is that the "Not-Good" list is much longer, and the
discussion of those preachers/characteristics is much livelier.

When Jerusalem met Athens, the "Thou Shalts and Shalt Nots" of the
Hebrew commandments met the Greek and Roman classical preoccupation
with virtues and vices. The Apostle Paul's lists provided a starting place for the
theologians of the church. In the sixth century, Pope Gregory I formed what
has become the definitive list of the seven deadly sins: lust, gluttony, greed,
sloth, wrath, envy, and pride. Of course, human vanity knows no bounds when
it comes to inventing new ways to be irresponsible. So the development of one
list led to forming another—a list of virtues. The virtues list named qualities
of character as habits church leaders wanted Christ's followers to cultivate. Did
that leave any room for the gifts and graces of the Spirit, or were they walking down that Pelagian path? They came up with two lists. One identified four
cardinal virtues: prudence, justice, temperance, and courage, which were to be
developed by human effort. The other added three theological virtues infused by
God: faith, hope, and charity/love.[6]

Needless to say, a list of the virtues and vices of preaching could be a very
long book. Although it is crucial to discuss and describe the habits and efforts of
preachers, we must also leave room for the gifts and graces of God. So, how did
we do this? We began by identifying the relevant theological measures and then
turning to the rhetorical tradition to identify communicative resources that can
serve either responsible or irresponsible ends.

Identifying Theological Measures

We believe that congregations want preachers whose pulpit practice is both
reliable and faithful. Should *reliability* be used as the term to measure theologically responsible versus irresponsible pulpit speech? And what of faithfulness?
There are several reasons why we believe that reliability and faithfulness taken
together are the right measures of theological pulpit practice. But let's begin by
identifying what's not at stake in their use.

What's Not in View?

Obviously there are theological pulpit practices that one tradition might
find responsible and another tradition may not view as either reliable or faithful. For example, the degree to which embellishment is encouraged or expressive
and stylistic presentational habits are or are not welcome in the pulpit varies
among theological traditions. Confessional practices differ in these matters as
well. People in some confessional traditions place greater trust in the ordained

status of clergy who have been trained in a denominational seminary and have been duly ordained by a bishop or some other authorizing agency of the church. People in other traditions place more trust in clergy who preach in ways that make it clear that a communally affirmed interpretation of the biblical text is the authorizing agency for a responsible theological pulpit practice. People who have participated in the worship of a congregation far from their own confessional experience or tradition often become acutely aware that these differences surface rather quickly as they ponder whether to trust what is communicated.

In addition, theologies per se differ in ways that are not a matter of ethics. Sacramental theology can differ at key points from Reformed theology; Anabaptist theology differs from Pentecostal theology. Conservative theologies differ from progressive ones. There are many resources that can help preachers consider what makes for reliable and faithful ways to interpret and communicate the theological commitments of their traditions. But reliability and faithfulness in such practices should not be considered an issue of ethics as much as an issue of adequacy or inadequacy in representing the perspective of the preacher's theology.

For example, the misstep identified in Bob's opening story occurred in the context of fundamentalist preaching. Many readers may have winced at the theology being preached, but that is not an issue of practical ethics; it's an issue of theology. We believe that missteps and irresponsible practice should be identifiable regardless of one's tradition or which theology is served by the preaching. As the measures we propose here, reliability and faithfulness are intended to be descriptions of a preacher's pulpit conduct. Irresponsible preaching as well as its responsible alternative should be identifiable regardless of differences in theology, confessional traditions, or styles of presentation. One of the challenges, therefore, is for you, the individual preacher, to join with us in this exploration to identify and recognize what, in your particular community, is theologically appropriate speech and what types of talk cross the line.

What Is in View?

So why did we choose reliability and faithfulness as our measures of ethical theological practice? First, they are the measures found in Scripture itself. Second, others have turned to them as useful criteria of trustworthy practice.

Reliability is the translation of the word *pistos* in biblical contexts in which the notion of trustworthiness as perceived by others is in view. For example, this is the primary term the Apostle Paul reverts to when it comes to his own resume (1 Cor. 4:8-13; 2 Cor. 4:8-9; 6:4-5; 11:23-29). "Think of us in this way," he writes to the Corinthians, "as servants of Christ and stewards of God's mysteries. Moreover, it is required of stewards that they be found trustworthy" (1 Cor. 4:1-2)—that they be found to be *pistos* by those who depend on them. Depending on context, this word is used to render the cluster of ideas of trustworthiness, reliability, faithfulness, conviction, belief, or believability.

"Faithfulness" is the translation of this same word in contexts in which commitment to God and God's purposes is in view. For example, in Galatians 3:9, Paul explains that Abraham was a person who had faith (*pisteuô*) and was also a person who was found to be faithful (*pistô*). It is this same quality of character, rather than pride of achievement, that Paul values in commending respect for colleagues such as Epaphras, Tychicus, and Onesimus; they were faithful as ministers of the gospel among the Colossian Christians (Col. 1:7; 4:7, 9). Whether to translate this as "reliable" or "faithful" is a matter of judgment and syntax; the former renders the notion of credibility in the eyes of others while the latter renders the notion of remaining true to God's purposes.

At one point Paul contrasts the character of his ministry with the ministries of those who try to please or persuade people by what he considers irresponsible means: "Take pride in those who minister with the right heart rather than the right look" (freely derived from 2 Cor. 5:12). This juxtaposition between the right heart versus the right look is core to a Christian ethics grounded in one's character having reliability for listeners and demonstrating faithfulness to the gospel. Rather than making choices that are outwardly acceptable or advantageous in the moment, the Christian leader is called to make choices from a servant-centered heart—from his or her character in Christ. As A. J. Gordon, founder of Gordon College, once said, "We do not stand in the world bearing witness to Christ, but stand in Christ and so bear witness to the world."[7]

Contemporary studies in the credibility of preachers have affirmed the centrality of a preacher's trustworthiness/reliability.[8] Credibility was the central measure in a significant qualitative study that sought to determine how it is that parishioners come to understand that sermons preached by their pastor can actually be the word of God for them.[9] Credibility is also the most important quality everyone looks for in their leaders (whether secular or sacred) as people we rely on to be honest, forward-looking, inspiring, and competent.[10] More than just someone to be counted on or someone who will be consistent, this conception of personal credibility is meant to identify those individuals who are faithful to inner resources of character.

Of course, secular studies tend to see the classic rhetorical element of reliability as a function of perceived credibility and make faithfulness an internal dimension of personal integrity—of being true to yourself. Those who are called to preach the gospel, however, understand that they serve as witnesses to something beyond this "look within" and the "look without" locus of authority. For our purposes, we believe the "look within" is the basis of ethical practice expressed as reliability when it comes to respect for listeners and the "look without" is faithfulness in respect to the gospel.

Reliability and faithfulness are the two theological measures—two sides of the same biblical idea—we will set in tensional juxtaposition in proposing a typology of practice-centered ethics in preaching. For the other measures of the typology we turn to the classical rhetorical tradition to provide a set of resources that permit distinctions in the virtues and vices of communicative pulpit practice.

Why Rhetoric?

According to Aristotle, rhetoric should be defined as the ability to see what is possibly persuasive in every given case.[11] That understanding has served well across two millennia of coming to understand what is at stake when we try to communicate our beliefs and commitments with others. It does not mean that a skilled communicator can always be persuasive. It simply means that, like a skilled physician who knows all the possible means that can be applied to aid a patient, a well-trained communicator should be aware of the possible means of achieving the most effective communicative purposes in a presenting situation.[12] In this sense, the classical understanding of rhetoric treats this art instrumentally as a specific set of resources available to achieve persuasive purposes.

More recent conceptions of rhetoric treat the art as intrinsic to human knowing itself. Since we employ language as a symbol-making system in order to communicate, contemporary theorists have come to realize that we use that same medium to arrive at all of our meaning-making. This second view of rhetoric means that dismissing rhetoric as nothing more than manipulative efforts to influence others, even when people use persuasion inappropriately, is naive. Rhetoric, for good or ill, is intrinsic to all the convictional understanding of our lives—to all reasoning. We can persuade ourselves to support worthy causes, or we can fool ourselves into believing that next time things will be better, but in all of this, human reasoning is rhetorical. We develop arguments to persuade others, to justify or clarify views we hold, and to explore whether something we think can sustain further examination. The resources we use to engage in the daily human processes of reasoning arise from a tradition where thinking logically, compassionately, and contextually all come together to help us shape convictions.

Something of this idea is captured in the word the New Testament uses to speak of our belief as faith. When Jesus says, "Those who believe in me, even though they die, will live, and everyone who lives and believes in me will never die" (John 11:25b-26a), the word rendered as *belief* is a version of the word *pistos* we have already encountered as a way to translate trustworthiness, reliability, and faithfulness. The idea of "believing in" something (to adhere to, to trust in, to rely on) in the New Testament is actually a form of the same word Aristotle and Plato used to talk about being persuaded or having convictions about some matter. A distinction we often make is between our belief (the basis of our convictions) versus our faith (the expressive activity we engage in based on those convictions). Of course we can treat faith like a noun rather than a

9

verb (e.g., "The faith that was once for all entrusted to the saints" [Jude 3]), but this is unusual in Scripture. For our purposes, the more recent ways of treating rhetoric as the intrinsic medium of human thought reflect this ancient correlation between conviction and faith in the New Testament.[13] And for this reason we believe it is natural to look to the resources of rhetoric to make virtue and vice distinctions in how it is that humans communicate with others about matters of faith.

We're not alone in returning again and again to the tradition of rhetoric to recover resources that can be used in proposing a virtue ethic. The contemporary rhetorician Wayne Booth recently proposed an ethics of virtuous rhetorical practice in his book *The Rhetoric of Rhetoric*. He argues that the choice of some people to irresponsibly engage in what he calls "rhetrickery" is not a justifiable reason to surrender our commitment to arrive at good and ethically responsible ways of gaining public assent for our convictions.[14] He contends that all encounters between the one who communicates and the audience are ethical because they are rooted in the character of the participants. Applied to preaching, this claim reminds us that preachers invite parishioners to keep company with them in sermons by creating a way of looking at the world.[15] With good sermons, convictions can change because of the experience of listening, especially when preachers are effective in naming God and naming grace in the lives of those who hear their words.[16] We look to this same tradition and turn to the classical resources of *ethos*, *pathos*, and *logos*—resources that help preachers imagine what is persuasively possible—as the means of distinguishing the virtues of responsible preaching from the vices of irresponsible pulpit practice.

A TYPOLOGY OF IRRESPONSIBLE PREACHING

Concern for responsible and irresponsible use of the rhetorical resources of *ethos*, *pathos,* and *logos* draws attention to the moral dimension of communicative practice. They can provide a virtue ethics of responsible and irresponsible preaching when juxtaposed to the two biblical measures of reliability for listeners and faithfulness to the gospel. The result produces a typology of six vices and six corresponding virtues for preaching practice.

Our "Irresponsible Preaching Typology" claims that failures of in-authenticity, greed, and exploitation represent a lack of reliability for listeners. Failures of self-absorption, pandering, and self-righteousness represent a lack of faithfulness to the gospel. In subsequent chapters we will take up these sins of pulpit practice that variously turn the preacher into a Pretender, an Egoist, a Manipulator, a Panderer, a Demagogue, or a Despot.

Irresponsible Preaching Typology			
	Failed Ethos	**Failed Pathos**	**Failed Logos**
Lack of Reliability for Listeners	The Pretender The Sin of In-Authenticity	The Manipulator The Sin of Greed	The Demagogue The Sin of Exploitation
Lack of Faithfulness to the Gospel	The Egoist The Sin of Self-Absorption	The Panderer The Sin of Trendiness	The Despot The Sin of Self-Righteousness

Our "Responsible Preaching Typology" provides a counterproposal of virtues that preachers should practice in order to be reliable for listeners by responding to the call to be genuine, to exercise self-control, and to woo a reasoned reception of the message preached. Similarly they should respond to the call to be selfless, to be honest to God, and to reveal the ineffability of God as practices that serve faithfulness to the gospel.

Responsible Preaching Typology			
	Responsible Ethos	**Responsible Pathos**	**Responsible Logos**
Reliabilizy for Listeners	Authentic The Call to be Genuine	Careful The Call to Exercise Self-Control	Courteous The Call to Woo a Reasoned Reception
Faithfulness to the Gospel	Humble The Call to be Selfless	Passionate The Call to be Honest to God	A "Namer of God" The Call to Reveal an Ineffable God

These virtues of pulpit practice form each chapter that follows as a preacher's vocational calling to become more Authentic, Careful, Courteous, Humble, Passionate, and a "Namer of God."

Ethos as a Moral Dimension

According to Aristotle, *ethos* functions as one of three means available to a speaker that can assist him or her in achieving a persuasive purpose with a specific audience or group of people. It is often translated as character or credibility, but in Aristotle's use it really applied more to what we might call persona. Contemporary notions of credibility are distinguished from persona because speakers are often introduced by someone well known to listeners. This individual vouches for that person's credentials and commends him or her to the listeners. *Ethos* as envisioned by Aristotle, however, is a more supple resource. It emerges during the speech as the persona evident in the speaker's *phronesis* (wisdom), the speaker's apparent *arete* (virtue), and the speaker's *eunoia* (goodwill directed toward listeners).[17] When these interests are juggled well, they function as a resource that heightens the willingness of a group of listeners to be receptive to the ideas and arguments a speaker presents. Handled poorly, the argument does not fare well regardless of how sound it is. According to Aristotle, if listeners do not trust the persona that a speaker manifests, they won't be persuaded by the content of what is said either.

Ethos is embodied in the interplay between what a speaker planned to say and what is actually communicated. As a result, listeners become disposed to see what a speaker says as an authentic expression of his or her goodwill, virtue, and wisdom, or they come to question whether these qualities are characteristic of the individual. The latter was a problem made keenly apparent in the story of England's King George VI, a story told in the film *The King's Speech*. King George had to overcome a problem of stammering in order for his radio addresses to be taken seriously by the British people during the war years. At issue for everyone concerned was the degree to which his stammering was a barrier to credibility.[18]

But more than just an issue of credibility, failed *ethos* can become irresponsible practice and a moral failure on the part of the preacher. Preachers who fail to maintain respect for listeners, who allow other concerns to overwhelm their task of regularly offering a reliable witness to their own faith, can easily become pretenders. Authentic preaching responds to the call to be communicatively genuine in all pulpit practices, engaging the voices of others, but remains true to a person's own convictions and experience of faith. Preachers become egoists when, in the name of proclaiming the gospel, they lose sight of being faithful to the gospel because they become self-absorbed. Faithfulness in preaching the gospel is a call to selflessness when it comes to who should receive praise. In chapters 2 and 3 we explore the vices of irresponsible ethos and the character of its virtuous expression for responsible preaching.

Pathos as a Moral Dimension

According to Aristotle, *pathos* has to do with how we get people to care about what we communicate. In his day, Aristotle was troubled over the misuse of pathos. He was concerned that crafty sophists were helping people bend the will of judges by making emotive rather than reasoned appeals. It was the equivalent of the modern-day practice of lawyers going for jury nullification, appealing to the compassion of jurors rather than presenting the evidence or relying on the law for their verdict. For Aristotle, the ability to appeal more to the emotive than the cognitive side of reasoning is the power of pathos. But rather than reject this ability, he grasped that what characterizes human judgment is the fact that we can be moved as well as convinced. Humans can find some things repugnant or even horrifying. We can find other things pleasurable and occasionally winsome. And it is the ability to be moved in this manner when combined with cognitive appeals that actually leads us to act.

It is this dual element of judgment, Aristotle argues, that permits humans to change their minds over time and change what their response might be even when faced with the same "evidence." Though normally termed the emotive dimension, pathos appeals have a moral dimension because they are intrinsic to this capacity that makes us human. One philosopher describes this moral dimension of pathos as Aristotle's deep psychological insight into the "everyday-ness of Being with one another."[19]

Of course, marketers, advertisers, and salespeople have long since realized that consumers are far more easily swayed by messages crafted to bypass reasoned argument. We think of this as manipulation when we question the motives of the one trying to sway us. Preachers who play to pathos in manipulative ways often lose sight of their calling to responsibly care for those with whom they share common community as the people of God. Or preachers who lose sight of remaining true to concerns and commitments of the gospel often discover that they have misplaced their passion by making appeals that play to the self-interest of what parishioners want to hear rather than what is honest to God. In chapters 4 and 5 we explore the vices of irresponsible pathos and the concerns of its virtuous expression for responsible preaching.

Logos as a Moral Dimension

As the third means available to influence people, reasoned argument is what most people think of when focusing on ways people are influenced by the content of what is communicated.[20] *Logos* refers to the linkages of reasoning in what gets said in preaching. The minister or priest makes a reasoned case for looking at or understanding a gospel implication in a certain way by making a claim in some manner and providing arguments that support it. This might look or sound like the Apostle Paul's carefully reasoned thought or his sagacious use of metaphor. For others this might look like John's use of poetic imagery or like Jesus' use of dialogue and parable. All of these are forms of reasoning and, therefore, forms of argument. They are presented as language shaped to woo listeners to be responsive to a specific way of understanding the ideas in view. These *logoi* are what Aristotle would consider artistic modes of reasoning employed to influence others.

Contemporary efforts to explore what counts as sound reasoning strategies for our time typically link this way of thinking about argument with efforts to persuade others. Of course for many people any use of the word *argument* still carries a negative connotation. The tension between these two ways of seeking to influence others reveals what's at stake in the moral dimension of this resource. Demagogues and Despots both tend to operate with an assumption that truth is a scarce resource and that they are the only ones who know the best way to direct its power. Demagogues become irresponsible by exploiting the beliefs and values of others to serve their own narrow or toxic view of faith. Despots become irresponsible when they self-righteously assume their version of the truth is the only truth.

Preachers can practice virtuous influence when they courteously work to woo a reasoned—rather than a demagogic-inspired—response to faith. They can practice faithfulness to the gospel when they learn how to Name God in the lives of people—by working to reveal the nature of an ineffable God who can never be fully comprehended by anyone's despotlike personal version of the truth. In chapters 6 and 7 we consider the vices of irresponsible logos and the quality of its virtuous expression for responsible preaching.

MISSTEPS, UNTHINKING MISTAKES, AND THE CALL TO VIRTUE

In chapter 8—"Wait! Wait! There's More!"—we explore missteps that are distinguished from irresponsible practice on one hand and unthinking mistakes on the other. We gather up some of the other problematic practices from teaching homiletics. As opposed to the six deadly or "mortal" sins in the previous chapters, we might think of these as the "venial" or forgivable sins of preaching.

Unthinking mistakes can occur easily but are problematic behaviors nonetheless. Missteps, like the one lifted up in opening story of this chapter, represent behavior in which the preacher is aware that she or he has chosen to accept or settle for an orientation that can become a habit in framing an approach to preaching. Developing negative habits such as this perpetuate patterns of behavior that can lead to irresponsible preaching practice.

In the epilogue chapter we will consider how coherence in the virtuous practices of preaching can lead to modeling a vision of responsible pulpit character capable of sustaining the *communio sanctorum* in a particular congregation. We believe that making choices grounded in the virtues of character should be a habit of intentional practice, something that a preacher should purposefully identify in developing his or her own credo in these matters.

Matters of Life and Death

When Lucy was working on a previous book she chose every occasion with fellow clergy to ask them what they wish that they had learned in their preaching classes and what they would want new preachers to know. On one of those occasions a friend and colleague came up to her and stood nose to nose. "I want you," he told her, "I want you to tell them that people are listening. Tell them that their preaching matters. Tell them that people take sermons seriously and that they, as preachers, should do that as well. This is no laughing matter."

We have written this book because we take preaching seriously and we take our teaching seriously. God calls preachers to a ministry that brings hope and the message of good news to people who sit in darkness. Your words matter. You matter. And we want to help you become the best preacher you can be. We want you to be a faithful, responsible preacher. Our purpose is neither to scold nor chastise. We do not want to frighten you. In fact, as the design of this book suggests, we are aware there is a sense of what the British would call cheekiness in declaring six ethical failures to be the great sins of preaching. We don't think our list is exhaustive. Nor are we trying to reassert the language of mortal and venial sins for all confessional traditions. So we are serious and occasionally a bit playful. What we offer is a start at identifying what should count as responsible and irresponsible pulpit conduct. Our hope is that you read and think about this list of sins in a similar manner. Our desire is to call readers to become ethically responsible for the faith we proclaim by naming the sins of overreaching and by directing attention to the practices that build homiletic character.

Are you going to make mistakes? Are you going to step over the line into irresponsible preaching? Yes. We know because we have done it ourselves. But we also know that we have been called to preach by a gracious, understanding, and forgiving God who is there to pick us up when we fall and set us back on the right path.

We want to help you begin to recognize the potential sins, and the lines in the sands of preaching, so that you will be faithful to God, to the gospel, and to the people to whom God has called you to serve.

FOR FURTHER READING

Stephen Seamands. *Ministry in the Image of God: The Trinitarian Shape of Christian Service.* Downers Grove, IL: IVP Press, 2005.

Barbara Brown Taylor. *The Preaching Life.* Cambridge: Cowley Press, 1993.

William H. Willimon. *Calling and Character: Virtues of the Ordained Life.* Nashville: Abingdon Press, 2000.

N. T. Wright. *After You Believe: Why Christian Character Matters.* San Francisco: HarperOne, 2010.

Chapter Two

THE
PRETENDER

When Rebekah overheard her husband, Isaac, preparing to give their older twin, Esau, his dying blessing, she realized it was time to garner that privilege for the younger twin, and her favorite, Jacob. Isaac's eyesight had failed and he was forced to rely only on his other senses. So as Esau went off to prepare the savory meal his ailing father had requested, Rebekah roasted two young goats and placed their skins on Jacob's arms. Unlike those of his twin, Jacob's arms were smooth, and with the goat skins he pretended to be his brother. Isaac was confused. He heard Jacob's voice but felt Esau's arms. When the pretender claimed that he was Esau, Isaac decided that it must be so and he bestowed the blessing reserved for the elder on the younger. Needless to say, this deception carried consequences.

History is filled with the stories of people who pretended to be another. When the decision was made to turn the musical *My Fair Lady* into a movie, everyone assumed that songbird Julie Andrews, who had achieved great success in the Broadway production, would step into the cinema version. Although costar Rex Harrison reprised his role as Professor Higgins, Andrews did not make the cut. Rather, Audrey Hepburn was cast as Eliza. As audiences settled into their seats it was the beautiful Hepburn who appeared as the bedraggled flower seller singing, "All I want is a room somewhere . . ." If movie lore is correct, unbeknownst to even Hepburn, all of Eliza's songs were dubbed by soprano Marni Nixon, who is not mentioned in the credits. It was Marni, not Audrey, who trilled that she could have danced all night.

This was not the first time that Marni Nixon was the uncredited voice behind the star. Rather than that of star Deborah Kerr, Marni's voice sang with Yul Brynner in *The King and I*. In the motion picture adaptation of *West Side Story*, neither of the principal stars could sing well. When Richard Beymer and Natalie Wood sing to each other on the fire escape balcony, their voices belong to Jimmy Bryant and Marni Nixon. Again, they were uncredited.

Did Deborah Kerr, Natalie Wood, or Audrey Hepburn get into trouble for "pretending" to have beautiful voices? Hardly. In their case, the decision was out of their control. The same cannot be said for preachers who pretend to be someone else.

As we noted in the opening chapter, Lucy invites her students to reflect upon and develop lists describing the qualities of "good" and "not-good" preaching. Each year traits such as boring, too academic, and judgmental make it on the list (don't worry, we will return to those). What never makes the list? A mortal sin from which many offenders are never able to recover: plagiarism.

Why do Lucy's students never include plagiarism on the not-good list? It is because, like moviegoers enjoying Marni Nixon's version of Eliza Doolittle's songs, they often are unaware that the preacher is pretending to be someone else. They do not realize that they are listening to borrowed testimony.

Professor Rick Lischer of Duke Divinity School and Bishop Noel Jones of the Greater Bethany Church in Los Angeles were interviewed on the subject of "sermon slippage" as guests on Tavis Smiley's National Public Radio program.[1] In response to a question concerning the quality of sermons today and the problem of plagiarism, Lischer noted that preachers have always made use of the writings of others. Unfortunately, the Internet has made it too easy to cross an ethical line between legitimate borrowing and inauthentic appropriation. For Lischer, the real problem arises when someone downloads and uses the very words of another, representing the ideas and experiences as if they were his or her own. "Part of the genius of preaching," Lischer said, "is that a preacher reaches down into his or her own soul to craft a message. If a preacher is overly reliant on the ideas and language of others, there is a certain lack of authenticity."[2]

As a case in point, Smiley turned to Bishop Jones and asked whether he was flattered or frustrated by the fact other ministers were "borrowing" his sermons and preaching them as their own. Jones responded that, of course, he was flattered on one hand, but on the other hand it had also created problems of a different kind. Jones's sermons are produced and distributed on tapes and CDs that can be purchased. On one occasion he was invited to preach for a midwestern congregation. The pastor who picked him up at the airport was effusive in his praise for Jones's pulpit ministry and told him that he used Jones's sermons all the time. He was proud of the fact that he delivered the sermon so close to the style of Jones that he had the timing and nuance of every "Hallelujah!" at exactly the same point as it was in the original. As Jones recounted this, there was knowing laughter from both Lischer and Smiley. On the way in from the airport the preacher asked Jones what he planned to preach.

> "Well, I am going to preach [the sermon] 'A Word for Your Situation.'" And he said, "You can't do that." . . . And I said, "I can't do that? What do you mean?" [laughter] And he said, "Do you have something else?" [Strong laughter in which Jones joins.] And I said, "Well, yeah. Okay. I'll do, 'He's My God, Too.'" And he said, "You

18

can't do that one either." [More joint laughter.] And I said, "Why can't I preach this?" I had to pull something out that had not yet been out on cassettes or CDs because he had preached it all.[3]

Jones went on to note that this is a growing problem, especially for pastors of larger congregations. The leadership demands of what for some have become multimillion-dollar corporations have overshadowed the time necessary to produce quality sermons.

There can only be one reason that the minister was so insistent that Jones's sermons couldn't be repreached. But does the time crunch and the need to be effective justify misrepresenting authenticity when preaching? Obviously, this is an egregious example of irresponsible preaching, but the more disturbing element, below the nervous laughter in the interview, is that it was so blatant. It suggests that the problem is far more prevalent than one might assume.

Of course, in southern preaching and especially in black preaching there is a tradition of doing riffs on famous sermons. It is a form of sampling, engaging the form of well-known set pieces both as homage to the preacher and as an opportunity to distinguish oneself in the royal lineage of that sermon. But the preacher who was hosting Bishop Jones knew he had done more than a riff on this man's sermons. He had stolen them and presented them as his own. In the name of being effective he had sacrificed the congregation's need for him to be authentic. And rather than offering his own witness to faith in God he had become a pretender, offering borrowed perceptions rather than original conceptions in God's name.

THE PRETENDER AND THE PROBLEM OF IN-AUTHENTICITY

There is significant pressure on preachers today to energize, engage, and entertain listeners while also sharing profound insight. Every Sunday. The commitment people once had to a particular community of faith increasingly has given way to the individualistic desire to hear the word of God from someone who seems to be able to articulate a compelling witness to faith. As Pastor Tim Keller of Redeemer Presbyterian Church in New York City observes, contemporary people are far less loyal to a congregation, a denomination, or even a particular theological tradition. What they want is a great Sunday experience. Whether it's excellent worship or a gifted preacher they will travel to experience it. Add this kind of pressure to a typical pastor's busy week and the accessibility of so much sermon material available through the Internet and "the temptation to simply re-preach someone else's sermon is very strong."[4]

We live in a media-rich environment in which excellence in thought and in production values for visual media is at our fingertips. Protestant clergy preach in a tradition that historically has placed great weight on the sermon, while Catholicism has placed its emphasis on the liturgy of the Mass. But since Vatican II placed more emphasis on the homily, even Catholic clergy are facing the need to deal with the expectation that preaching matters. Likewise, clergy in every tradition now find themselves in competition with other clergy who have become adept in the use of a variety of digital resources in preaching. Add to this the competitive nature of attracting parishioners if a congregation is to thrive and the pressure for sermons is to be not just good but really good. It is a seductive pressure because those who give in to its attractions can find themselves becoming people who have let the means become the end, letting effectiveness trump authenticity. And if they give in to a regular diet of "heavy lifting" in the pulpit, they may come to realize that in matters of witnessing to their faith, what they have become is a pretender.

In March 2002, members of Christ Church Cranbrook near Detroit accused its minister of delivering sermons verbatim from a lectionary sermon source on the Internet. Christ Church is a sizable congregation that makes significant demands on its rector's time and leadership. Even as we write almost a decade later, this episode is still the most well-known challenge to repreaching someone else's sermons explored in the national press. When this "borrowing" became public, the congregation's leadership suspended the minister for three months while they determined how to proceed with their concerns. The parishioners were frankly troubled that he could pass off as his own the ideas, experiences, and the words of someone else. However, the Internet lectionary service from which he downloaded his sermons fully grants permission to copy and share any of its material in oral use without regard to attribution. We should note that the lectionary resource supplier instigated no action against him; it was the congregation who were troubled.

Is this kind of problem a sign of a lapse of character or just the sign of an overworked pastor whose congregation expects too much originality? Is it really plagiarism if the Internet provider grants the verbatim rights to use the material?

The congregation allowed him to remain at his parish. As Lucy mentioned in the opening chapter, one of her colleagues encountered a similar situation. A new pastor arrived at National City Christian Church in Washington, DC, with the reputation as a great preacher. In 2003, a parishioner Googled the title of her pastor's upcoming sermon. Much to her surprise a sermon with the same title had been preached by Thomas Tewell of Fifth Avenue Presbyterian Church in New York. She was able to print out the sermon and sit with it in her lap as her pastor preached Tewell's sermon, word for word. She reported her discovery to church officials, and they quickly discovered that he had been "borrowing" sermons for over a year and a half. He took a ten-week leave of absence, hoping that there would be forgiveness and reconciliation.

There is little wrong with borrowing insights from various resources for Sunday's sermon. In fact, it is a healthy practice. Good sermons arise as part of the preacher's dialogue with Scripture, with potential listeners, reflection on personal experience, engagement with a theological tradition, sounding the culture's questions, and with the published efforts of other preachers on the subject or the text. Excellence in preaching is evidenced by personal engagement with a variety of these voices. Temptation arises with the idea to do more than just engage them. When borrowing becomes verbatim preaching, as in the cases described above, this kind of "misrepresentation" may be grounds for suspension and perhaps even dismissal. In the end, both the minister and the Cranbrook congregation weathered their storm together and he served the parish for another seven years.[5] Unfortunately, the other pastor was overcome by the furor created by his borrowing and chose to resign. But in many congregations, the practice of preaching the sermons of others is increasing.[6]

Borrowing or Kidnapping?

What is plagiarism? Generally, it is considered to be an unauthorized act of intentionally copying someone else's ideas, whether spoken or written, and presenting them as original work. *The Oxford Dictionary of Literary Terms* notes, "Plagiarism is not always easily separable from imitation, adaptation, or pastiche, but is usually distinguished by its dishonest intention." In reality, there is a lot of borrowing and influence that goes on in the production of anything worth reading or hearing. That is a good thing. Once the term *plagiarism* is applied to borrowing, however, it suggests a large amount of uncited, verbatim usage rather than just influence. It also reframes the activity as a form of cheating. In educational settings, students who download their papers, copy them from hoarded fraternity files, or borrow them from a friend's hard drive are cheating. When caught they typically claim they were too busy to write an original assignment. Of course, the purpose of an academic exercise is originality of authorship. So is originality of authorship truly a requirement of preaching? Is this a fair comparison?

One pastor reported, in a later interview, that he felt overwhelmed by his responsibilities at the church and his leadership role at the denominational level: "It's a pattern you get into . . . It happens bit by bit. You end up using more and more. You're using a little material maybe initially and then using more. It's really not rational."[7] Pastor Rick Warren of Saddleback Community Church urges preachers to freely repreach the material he develops without getting bogged down in issues of attribution or contribution. When a pastor called to apologize for having preached one of his sermons, Warren responded that his sermons were posted for a reason: "Buddy, that's the point!" For Warren, the witness is in the words, not who says them.[8] It is the witness, not the watermark that matters. Of course, it's unlikely that Warren assumed a preacher would repreach his sermons word for word.

Whether it's using a Saddleback sermon outline or a full sermon provided by a lectionary resource, Tom Long suggests that this way of thinking represents a cultural shift from a proprietary to an open-source orientation to ideas. Open-source preaching means that the one who originated the words has already blessed their free use by others. Long doesn't buy the argument. "Giving credit to others is not merely a matter of keeping our ethical noses clean," he suggests. "It is also a part of bearing witness to the gospel."[9] Long's point of view is more in keeping with the understanding of the original Greek word appropriated for plagiarism: "to kidnap."

So who should have the right to claim foul here? The one from whom the material was lifted? Or those to whom the material was presented as original reflection? Do congregations have a right to expect brilliant thoughts from a pastor every week while parish responsibilities keep multiplying? Is the reputation of the gospel as truth being put on the line by this habit? There seems to be little agreement about the ethics of this practice of borrowing or what others view as kidnapping in contemporary Christian preaching. In some congregations the parishioners may be only too glad that their pastor has found a way to have something of quality to say on Sunday morning—even if it is "appropriated" from another source rather than his or her own reflection. There is a reason most churches do not have a contractual statement forbidding preachers from borrowing the words of others.

Respect for Listeners

Some years ago a columnist in the *New York Times* suggested an interesting response to a question submitted to his column, "The Ethicist." A woman in Mableton, Georgia, wrote to say that her parish had just discovered that their senior pastor had been preaching the sermons of others. After assuring her that it was, indeed, unethical for the pastor to preach another's sermon without attribution, he then offered an unusual suggestion: "Perhaps sermon writing should not be a job requirement."[10] He went on to argue not only that clergy were very busy, but also that not all clergy were, well, gifted as writers or preachers. Therefore, a clergyperson might inform the congregation of that fact and assure them that she or he would find wonderful, engaging, challenging sermons by others and deliver them each Sunday. What would be crucial, he noted, would be that the listeners would know that she or he had not composed that sermon.

Historically, the church has always encouraged the act of "sampling" the work of other preachers. Preaching is supposed to be about the message, not who said the words first.[11] For example, shortly after Christians in England severed their ties with Rome, the Archbishop of Canterbury, Thomas Cranmer, recognized that preaching would be an important way to develop and publish the new understanding of church and what it would mean to be the Church of England. He also realized that he could not trust his clergy, for both their theology and their preaching skills were woefully lacking. Therefore, he published *The Book of Homilies*, a collection of sermons written primarily by Cranmer himself. The clergy were instructed to read those sermons rather than deliver their own. That certainly might qualify as "heavy lifting" except for the fact that parishioners knew it was happening.

Preaching at its best is always a collaborative venture rather than an isolated activity. The question for some preachers is, where is the line between influence, borrowing, and "heavy lifting"? For others, the question is not one of distinguishing between contribution and attribution; it's an issue of admitting that significant portions of their sermons are really just a collection of material taken from a variety of sources.[12]

Most preachers recognize the inappropriate ethical lapse of simply preaching someone else's sermon verbatim as their own without attribution (or even with it). No one wants to be a huckster. But we live in a culture in which speeding five miles an hour over the limit is the norm; because we are human, we are tempted to speed in sermons, too. So, after a week with too many demands, many preachers naturally turn to a lectionary source, not just for insight, but for the words of the sermon itself. They add to this a few other insights derived from the latest spiritually related book, CD, or podcasts. Then they top this off with some pithy statements from the other sermons they read as research. Some preachers are able to keep this at the level of influence, some borrow quite a bit, and for some the cobbled-together result is simply a pastiche of "heavy lifting" from these sources with only a smattering of original thought from the preacher. With tongue firmly in cheek, John Indermark suggests that these preachers may want to consider rephrasing the prayer before such sermons as, "May the words of Frank Smith's mouth and the meditations of Mary Wright's heart, be acceptable in your sight, O God."[13]

Perhaps the most telling question in this issue is whether, given the right context, preachers who preach the sermons of others verbatim or engage in heavy lifting from those sermons would be comfortable acknowledging that "most of today's message is a version of a sermon on this text preached by John Indermark." If preachers, like Bishop Noel Jones's host, are nervous over the possibility of parishioners realizing how much of their sermon was borrowed, then preaching pastiche sermons without acknowledgment is pretense even if it is effective.

Rhetorically, plagiarism is a problem of failed ethos. When it becomes a pattern of behavior in preaching, the preacher becomes a pretender, a person who plagiarizes the faith of others and presents it as his or her own. The pretender tries to connect with listeners by way of borrowed faith and borrowed witness. Over time it becomes a habit of in-authenticity. The pretender often confuses a passion to be effective (an end) with work that needs to be perceived as a reliable witness (a means).

The goal needs to be reliability, not effectiveness. Reliability in this instance entails communicating the authenticity of his or her own witness to faith. The preacher who goes down this road of pretense in the name of expediency offers sermons that, by definition, lack the ring of truth. Jamie Buckingham once wrote, "If it is not our own, if we have not experienced the truth we are preaching, how can we minister life to others? We need to do much more than plagiarize. We must grapple, ourselves, with the meaning that others have illuminated."[14] Failed ethos in matters like this often blinds individuals, in the name of being overextended or exhausted, to their own capacity to fake their engagement of faith in God.

THE VIRTUE OF AUTHENTICITY

Good sermons arise as part of the preacher's dialogue with a variety of resources. Excellence engages sources; plagiarism embezzles them. As Carter Shelly maintains, preachers need to develop a clear ethic that distinguishes between inspired reframing and outright "borrowing," between responsible influence and irresponsible plagiarism.[15] Like many pastors, Shelly has struggled with the possibility that on weeks when ministry demands make it almost impossible to do justice to the text, it is tempting to consider just preaching someone else's insight on the text—as long as the congregation is informed, of course. But she then ruminates on the question: do we move from pretense to virtue by simply informing the congregation that we are preaching a great sermon or one that comes from a lectionary resource?

Striving to be authentic matters even on those weeks when ministry intrudes on sermon-preparation time. Shelly arrives at five virtues embodied in offering one's own rather than someone else's witness: authenticity, immediacy, originality, credibility, and creativity. We agree, adding only that we believe authenticity is the collective expression of the other four virtues of becoming responsible for the faith we proclaim. We take them up in turn.

Immediacy

Shelly maintains that, when viewed as an active encounter, preaching establishes a quality of immediacy and relevancy in a sermon. It is this eventfulness of preaching the gospel that makes possible an experience of the word of God. For Shelly, preaching someone else's witness calls into question whether the sermon can become the word of God if the preacher is performing someone else's witness. Notice that Shelly frames the quality of immediacy in the language of the eventfulness of preaching. Some homileticians embrace this language as central to understanding how authenticity is experienced in preaching. Other homileticians desire to shift the intention of preaching away from affecting personal transformation in favor of affecting spiritual formation. What is common to both ways (transformative vs. formative) of understanding preaching's purpose is that preaching is to be experienced as the word of God rather than simply as a relevant word or as an effective word. Whatever differences these two approaches have when it comes to the desired response to be evoked by the language of a sermon, they share a belief that it is the immediacy of a sermon that portends its possibility to be the word for them.

Immediacy as a characteristic of authenticity is not achieved through either stylistic artifice (through imitation) or disingenuous pretense (dissimulation). Both may achieve effects with listeners, but the means should not be confused with the ends. Immediacy only occurs through the preacher's dialogical engagement with what is to be preached offered as witness that names God and names grace for others. Preachers that desire to pursue the virtue of responsible ethos with respect for listeners strive for this kind of immediacy.

Originality

Listeners expect they will hear about the preacher's encounter with "God's word, Christ's witness, and the Holy Spirit's inspiration." Shelly adds here, "I'd rather take my knocks for a bad sermon of my own than get praised for the one I didn't write."[16] But, as noted above, there is significant disagreement over the issue of originality. Vineyard Pastor Steve Sjogren recently addressed the topic of using sermon ideas developed by others rather than doing original work with a text. Effectiveness, he maintains, should be more important than originality:

> We need to get over the idea that we have to be completely original with our messages, each and every week. In my mind there is a tremendous amount of pride (let's call it what it is) when we insist on being completely original as communicators. In our desire to give "killer messages" we are dishing out something far less. Think about it for a second: If you really were giving a killer message each week, would your church be the size that it is right now? Maybe you need to be open to doing things a different way.[17]

Sjogren argues that striving to be original will not grow large churches. The most effective pulpit communicators he knows do not preach their own messages and do not feel compelled to tell congregations when they are preaching someone else's message. Instead of spending thirty hours a week these preachers spend about fifteen hours on the sermon and draw almost three quarters of the material from insights arrived at by others. Supporting this view, Sjogren could have called on no less of an authority than Augustine. Augustine urges that preachers ill-equipped to speak would be wise to commit to memory and deliver great sermons by others as long as it is done without deception.[18] But Shelly could call on theologian Karl Barth, who urges preachers simply to be themselves in the pulpit and to "stand behind your own poverty!" rather than think you must take on some authoritative role or speak some words from others that add profundity to your own witness. "We must not slip into comedy in borrowed robes," Karl Barth advises.[19]

In the contemporary debate, Sjogren would likely challenge Shelly's claim—"I'd rather take my knocks for a bad sermon of my own than get praised for the one I didn't write"—as an expression of pride. And Shelly might respond that she is not in the business of delivering "killer messages" in order to grow a large congregation.[20] For his part, Augustine's advice on originality may serve as the most apt arbiter in a question that is often one of degree of reliance—"as long as it is done without deception."

Credibility

Trust once breached, especially if the pastor does not acknowledge the borrowing, is not easily recovered. If parishioners discover that a pastor cannot be trusted to be reliable in his or her pulpit practice, the question arises where else the corners are being cut without acknowledgment. If the preacher's reliability is undermined because he or she has been irresponsible in this pretense, the question becomes: "What else may be pretense?"

It's one thing for a preacher to acknowledge that the morning's sermon is part of a series that the congregation is pursuing during which everyone is aware that the outlines for the sermon were generated by nationally known authors. As Tom Long notes, it's another thing for a preacher to admit that it was a busy week so she or he decided to preach someone else's famous sermon. Long says, "The air would go out of the room." The tacit agreement of preaching one's own testimony would be violated. This is why, Long contends, "that plagiarists, for all their blather about God's words being free for all, never confess their true sources and always imply that these words are coming straight from their heart."[21] The credibility of their own witness is always involved whenever a sermon is preached.

The challenge with becoming overly dependent on material developed by others is that it can quickly and easily become a search for the ideal message rather than one's own witness to faith. Or it can simply become a substitute for honestly taking up the questions posed by a text or the theology at stake in an issue. In either case, over time, a preacher who becomes too dependent on others can begin to detach from a personal witness and develop a preference to perform the witness of others.

Attributions, sparingly provided in sermons, add to the credibility of sermons. They provide a sense that the preacher has been able to find support that resonates with the material of the sermon. It takes very little to introduce an idea with, "It's been said that . . ." or "One writer has suggested . . . " or to actually name an individual from whom material is borrowed. The challenge for some preachers is to learn to let go of the need to document everything like they did in a seminary class. They must learn to speak with their own voice. The best writers and best preachers all draw on insights from others, incorporating them into their own engagement. When it comes to preaching, however, we do well to save full documentation for footnotes if texts are published on a website.

Creativity

Contemporary church blogger Ed Stetzer avoids weighing in on whether preaching someone else's sermons is plagiarism. What he has determined for himself is "that this practice was not spiritually healthy for me or for my church. It amounts to a kind of lip-syncing that robs not only a church of a truly prophetic voice but also a pastor of his own necessary development."[22]

When a preacher begins to develop an "excessive dependence" on the thoughtful reflection of others, in Shelly's words, it "stultifies" his or her own creativity in cultivating the practice of preaching. If the requirements of ministry in a given week make it impossible for a minister to develop a sermon, the question may need to be asked, "Has my preferred way of composing a sermon become an impediment rather than an aid to my creativity when faced with a time crunch?" If the need to have a "killer message" begins to outweigh the ability to wrestle with the text, then a preacher may need to ask, "Have I become someone who performs the witness of other people's faith rather than my own because I believe effectiveness matters more than personal authenticity?"

The challenge with the latter, of course, is that it begins with effectiveness as the purpose of preaching rather than witness that names God and names grace for others. Expediency, whether the goal is effectiveness or adequacy, should never be a palliative for the effort of honest witness. Creativity becomes a virtue that characterizes authenticity when preachers learn to become free of the fear that having the right word or having the best word is their responsibility. The preacher is the one who is responsible to name God and to name grace for others, not someone they read that week.

The Virtue of an Authentic Witness

What matters creatively should be a preacher's voice. In drawing together multiple resources for a sermon, they need to be filtered through the preacher's identity and the preacher's experience of faith in God. Over time parishioners come to see their pastor's passions, convictions, interests, questions, sensibilities, and affirmations as familiar perspectives. More than just reflecting his or her identity as a person of faith, they are present as that person seeks to be "real" about matters of faith.

Striving for authenticity in preaching is characterized by learning to cherish the virtues of facilitating immediacy, preferring originality, protecting credibility, and embracing creativity. In this way preachers can be said to be striving for authenticity in being respectful of their listeners. It is the authenticity of a preacher's voice week in and week out that is at the heart of faith formation for the *communio sanctorum*. If that voice is insufficiently one's own over time, then the faith that is formed from it lacks cohesiveness, not just for the preacher, but for the community as well. For this reason authenticity in creating what is finally offered as the word of God for listeners matters.

FOR FURTHER READING

Anna Carter Florence. *Preaching as Testimony*. Louisville, KY: Westminster John Knox Press, 2007.

Thomas G. Long. "Stolen Goods: Tempted to Plagiarize." *Christian Century* (April 17, 2007): 19–20

Carter Shelly. "Preaching and Plagiarism: A Guide for Introduction to Preaching Students." *Homiletic* 27, no. 2 (2002): 1–13.

Chapter Three

THE
EGOIST

An article in *Texas Monthly* magazine asks, "All his life, Joel Gregory strove to become pastor of Dallas' First Baptist Church. What torments then drove him to cast aside his position as the most powerful Baptist in the land and mysteriously flee from his pulpit?"[1] On November 25, 1990, Gregory had been unanimously chosen as the third pastor of what many considered to be the most influential Baptist pulpit in the nation. Though not the largest Baptist congregation in the country (in the 1990s, it averaged about 7,600 people in weekend services), it certainly qualified as one of the original mega-churches that emerged at the close of the twentieth century. Its influence and the influence of W. A. Criswell among Baptists in Texas went unquestioned.

In his book *Too Great a Temptation: The Seductive Power of America's Super Church*, Gregory answers the question. He tells a familiar story of a retiring pastor with almost fifty years of ministry having difficulty relinquishing the pulpit to a naive preacher who, with stars in his eyes, did not clarify when the retiring senior pastor would actually leave before accepting an appointment as the new senior pastor.[2] When Gregory came to realize that a two-month transition was about to become a four-year transposition of the hiring agreement, he abruptly resigned.

Gregory had to face how to remain a person of faith while living in what he describes as the "shadow of unguarded ego."[3] On the evening of his resignation, during which he had summarily "divested" himself of what most people would have believed to be "a religious empire," he realized he was walking away from what most clergy "would have paid any price, undergone any struggle, and faced any contempt to keep."[4] He remembered "the years of labor, study, obscurity, fatigue, and work that had brought me from nowhere to such a place. It was all gone with the wind of one night. And that was alright with me."[5] He respected Criswell, but he had no desire to engage in a duel of egos with the man who was considered by many to be one of the great princes of the twentieth-century pulpit. He had come to realize the toll it would take in making him an egoist as well. He writes, "When ego, competition, recognition, and manipulation invade, the pastor as master no longer works for the cause of Christ."[6]

There is nothing inherently wrong with being the pastor of a mega-church, he notes, but finding a way to be selfless while serving this kind of congregation becomes increasingly difficult unless the pastor is very intentional about acting responsibly. Time away from an active pulpit practice permitted Gregory to regain his perspective. In 2005, he became Professor of Preaching at Truett Theological Seminary at Baylor University.

THE EGOIST AND THE PROBLEM OF SELF-ABSORPTION

When it comes to preaching, the egoist is a person who is guilty of the vice of self-absorption. We were tempted to call this person an *egotist*—a person generally thought to have an inflated sense of his or her own importance or who tends to speak and write about issues in ways that privilege his or her personal thoughts, feelings, and experiences. But we chose to label this vice as egoism to be more inclusive. Egoists operate with self-interest as the guiding principle for their decision-making. They are more interested in power than privilege. Egoists begin with the need at hand and what they believe needs to happen or to occur in order to achieve the ends they believe necessary. But where most egotists are generally aware that they have made their own experience the touchstone of decision-making, egoists are often unaware that they operate in a world in which they have determined that good ends should justify whatever means it takes. In other words, egotists are always egoists, but not all egoists are egotists.

Those who teach homiletics well know the comment often scribbled in the margins of too many student sermons: "It's not about you. It's about the gospel!" Lucy recently had a student who, as the class prepared to discuss the sermon he had just preached, announced to his colleagues that he had been charged by his field education pastor not to talk about himself in his sermons. At the time, Lucy thought that this was an interesting requirement. The class then discussed the student's sermon. Later Lucy was able to read the sermon that he had previously delivered to his field education parish. She finally understood the reason for the pastor's directions. That sermon had been all and only about the student himself, his faith journey, his crises, and his questions about what he was doing.

In preaching, we affirm that it is God who gathers the community, who in the power of the Spirit blesses and sends people forth to continue the work of Christ in the world. This trinitarian perspective on preaching must come first. But egoists can become so self-absorbed with the leadership tasks of ministry, the crises and concerns of the faith community, or with their own need to advance some interpretive agenda, that the gospel becomes marginalized.[7]

We will look at two egoist temptations here. The first temptation is being seduced by the potential power of the pulpit. The second and perhaps more common temptation is that of becoming the moralizing autobiographer. Both vices produce preachers who end up at "cross-purposes" with the gospel.[8]

The Seductive Temptations of Pulpit Eloquence

The ambition and the fame that comes with becoming a prince or princess of the pulpit is something that must be negotiated prayerfully. Each person will handle it differently. If not engaged with true humility, it can turn an individual into a self-promoter rather than someone who selflessly proclaims the gospel. The distinction here is captured in the seemingly sage counsel, "There are two ways to preach: one way is to stand in front of the Cross and magnify yourself; the other is to lift up the Cross and keep yourself out of sight."[9] That seems simple enough: don't be at cross-purposes when preaching the gospel! But what does that look like?

Does this mean eloquence in the oral and physical delivery of a sermon is somehow something to be avoided in favor of delivering christological content? No. People will travel far to hear someone who can communicate the gospel with great effectiveness. They grasp that great preaching is eloquent in the power of what gets communicated, in the way it gets communicated, and in the way it serves as testimony by the one who speaks. The most famous definition of preaching, offered by Phillips Brooks in 1877, maintains that "preaching is the communication of truth by man to men. It has two essential elements, truth and personality. . . . Preaching is the bringing of truth through personality."[10] According to Brooks, if either of these two elements is sacrificed, then it is not preaching. Preaching is grounded in the incarnation. The Word became flesh and God continues to speak through our flesh. Brooks's conception likely has endured in part because of its artful balance of the human and the divine. It also may have endured because it balances logos as truth, ethos as personality, and pathos as the connective work found in the "bringing" event of preaching. Our point is that great preaching embodies truth as witness, which means maxims that challenge preachers to stay "out of sight" of the cross can create more confusion than illumination.

The most seductive aspect of preaching the gospel is the kind of power that accrues to the person who does it well—the power of personal acclaim, personal mastery, and personal magnetism. One does not have to ascend to heights of national prominence to have experienced the enticements that arise from wielding the power of a message delivered in a manner that has life-changing implications for others. Paul tells us "the gospel . . . is the power of God for salvation to everyone who has faith" (Rom. 1:16). And far from a spirit of timidity, preachers understand what it is like to experience the preaching moment as an expression of "a spirit of power and of love and of self-discipline" (2 Tim. 1:7).

In his treatise "The Priesthood," John Chrysostom was concerned that preachers' heads were being turned when listeners applauded. He wrote that preachers must be "indifferent to praise." This applause was overwhelming their passion for the gospel "because through his passion for praise he aims to speak more for the pleasure than the profit of his hearers."[11]

Preaching is powerful. This experience of power may be the very "power of God" at work, but it also is a power invoked by the words and testimony of the preacher. Typically we think of power as involving the possibility of imposing one's will on the behavior of others. Or we may think of it as involving the creation of a context by words well spoken through which others can become liberated from some form of domination. From a Christian perspective, we believe that this experience of power can be the work of redemption in the life of one who believes. What portion of this is the power of God and what portion is the power of the preacher cannot be defined.

The egoist is the preacher who has lost his or her way in this tensional dance between the power of the preacher and the power of craft. Egoists have become tempted by the power of the pulpit in ways that put them at cross-purposes with the pulpit's message. Preachers wield power in the pulpit, but that power must always be countercultural and other-directed. What the world saw as an instrument of death, an obscenity meant to scar the landscape, became for Paul and for the followers of Jesus the symbol of life, of hope, of resurrection, and of eternal life. The cross, André Resner reminds us, is meant to serve "as the lens of critical discernment for the church over against the world's ways of knowing and valuing."[12]

Preachers who lose their way and become seduced by a growing ability to move and influence people can become irresponsible if they become enamored more by their own power to use words well spoken than by "the power of God for salvation to everyone who has faith"—a power that comes through the preaching of the gospel (Rom. 1:16). Whether they build a reputation by providing triumphalist answers that attract increasing numbers of listeners or by some other message that brings acclaim, preachers must keep the counsel of Paul dear to their hearts:

> I did not come proclaiming the mystery of God to you in lofty words or wisdom. For I decided to know nothing among you except Jesus Christ, and him crucified . . . , not with plausible words of wisdom, but with a demonstration of the Spirit and of power, so that your faith might rest not on human wisdom but on the power of God. (1 Cor. 2:1-5)

Regardless of the size of the congregation, when a preacher develops a taste for being the recipient of acclaim as the one who can reveal mysteries to those hungering for meaning, it can become easy to embrace "the way of the world" rather than "the way of the cross." The temptation is great, since our culture suggests that recognition is due to those who seem able to gather a following.

32

A quarter century ago, in *The Culture of Narcissism*, Christopher Lasch argued that American culture quite literally teaches its citizens to obsess over becoming "successful" as an end rather than as a means. In effect, "the prevailing social conditions therefore tend to bring out narcissistic traits that are present in varying degrees in everyone."[13]

What Do We Do with Our Congregation's Praise?

Clergy are as susceptible as any to this pressure. How are we to respond to the comments at the church door, "Preacher, I just love your sermons. I only come to church because of you!" When trained to share a message that is quite literally liberating for others, preachers can readily find themselves adulated for this ability and can succumb to the belief that they should be rewarded and highly regarded for being the one who delivers this message. Sandy Hotchkiss, a psychotherapist who teaches in the School of Social Work at the University of Southern California, has identified what she calls the seven deadly sins of the narcissistic personality:

- Shamelessness—These individuals become self-promoting, having lost any sense that the work they lead is not all about them.
- Magical Thinking—These individuals have an increasing ability to cast any description of whatever has happened in light of how it affects their interests.
- Arrogance—These individuals assume that their interests, plans, and concerns are simply more important than those of anyone else.
- Envy—These individuals can have a disproportionate jealousy of the work of others whose recognition they believe should, by all rights, be theirs.
- Entitlement—These individuals believe due reward should come for whatever effort is expended.
- Exploitation—These individuals believe that it is the responsibility of others to make it possible for them to receive the reward for whatever effort is expended.
- Bad Boundaries—These individuals believe that boundaries are irrelevant if they stand in the way of their right to achieve the reward due their effort or their right to have their way.[14]

An Internet search quickly reveals an abundance of lay diagnostic analyses by people who believe their pastor is suffering from narcissistic personality disorder. They cite portions of the DSM-IV, the American Psychiatric Association's *Diagnostic and Statistical Manual of Mental Disorders,* fourth edition, in support of their contention. We believe that diagnosis should be left to the professionals, but the diagnostic manual does note that feelings of grandiosity combined with a lack of empathy and a willingness to exploit interpersonal relations for one's own benefit are central to this narcissistic behavior.[15] It's been said, with tongue in cheek, that concern that you might have this problem is likely an indication that you don't. We simply note that the opposite of the vice of narcissism is not self-deprecation; it is humility. Preachers are challenged, in all humility, to keep their ego in check as a way to be responsible in their pulpit practice. We will invite readers to take up the virtue of humility in the second half of this chapter, but one other temptation of ego in the pulpit needs to be addressed first.

The Common Temptation of Pulpit Autobiography

A cartoon in *Leadership Journal* once depicted a congregation cheerfully providing a pastor their gift of a massive multivolume series of books recounting all the stories he had told from the pulpit about himself, his wife, and his children. The cartoonist understandably depicted the pastor as bemused and a bit embarrassed by it all. There are differences of opinion by homileticians on the use of personal illustrations in the pulpit, but all agree that preachers must avoid the temptation to make themselves the hero of the gospel. When illustrating autobiographically it can become too easy to tell stories that indirectly become a proclamation of the virtuous preacher rather than the redemptive Christ. As preachers prepare sermons looking for ways to create identification with the subject matter being preached, it simply is easier to "strip-mine" their own lives for ready examples than to do the hard work of locating other material that makes the point. Most preachers would be shocked to realize that cumulatively this becomes a form of pulpit narcissism. When preaching in this manner, the preacher puts himself or herself at cross-purposes with proclaiming the gospel of a redemptive Christ.

No preacher plans to become a narcissist in the pulpit, but as these personal stories collect over time, parishioners learn to view the preacher as the hero who knows how to see God in action much better than they do. And it eventually seems to be the preacher who knows how to make the godly choice when faced with the dilemmas of life. Preachers may tell self-deprecating stories, but few preachers would actually tell stories about their own unresolved anger or lack of forgiveness. We become masters of the art of just the right kind of self-deprecation, which is often more rhetorical than real.

People love heart-warming stories, which is why there are endless versions of "chicken soup" books. As André Resner cannily observes, "People gobble up such stories like bite-sized brain candy, perhaps better, soul candy—high calorie, low nutrition."[16] When this occurs the very thing that makes the pastor so appealing to members of the congregation becomes a stumbling block for them to hear the counterculture message of the cross. We will return to this in the next chapter.

Two other ways preachers use personal stories irresponsibly are through privatism or isolationism.[17] Privatistic personal stories are those in which a preacher reveals personal information that has very little or really nothing to do with creating an interpretive identification for listeners. When it occurs, listeners often develop a split consciousness in which they leave the message of the sermon behind as they ponder the meaning of what the pastor has just revealed. Isolationist use of personal stories occurs when there is a complete disconnect between the purpose of the sermon and the purpose of the story. The latter may involve a preacher letting parishioners in on something that happened to him or her just last week. Or it may take the form of sharing heartwarming news in which the connection to the text is labored at best. Or worse, it may be a humorous anecdote the purpose of which is to warm up the crowd as if a sermon is a speech made before toastmasters. Each of these potential misuses of autobiographical material is an example of the egoist at work. When offered, autobiographical stories in sermons need to be vehicles that reveal the shape of the gospel through which the truth or discovery of the truth of the gospel should shine.[18]

A personal story can be a vehicle for Christian proclamation if used with care. Authenticity, the virtue that challenges the vice of pretense in preaching, eschews anonymity in the pulpit. The individual preaching stands before the congregation as a witness, and people want to hear how the gospel has intersected with the preacher's life. Students in writing classes are often taught to avoid the use of the first person pronoun in making claims, but when someone is speaking about something that matters to him or her personally, people long to hear indicators of personal reference. As Cardinal John Henry Newman once noted, "Nothing that is anonymous will preach."[19]

Bob recalls a time when a congregation made the painful decision to terminate the call of their pastor because he never shared anything personal from the pulpit. At first the laypeople thought that this might have been a style of preaching taught where he was trained for the ministry. The pastoral relations committee met with him and tried to explore this concern only to discover that he could not bring himself to speak personally about Christian faith in conversation either. He told them that he had been trained never to share personal stories in the pulpit. But they realized it wasn't just a question of the appropriateness of personal anecdotes in preaching. He presented teaching from the pulpit but did it in a manner more like someone educating them about the faith rather than someone who lived it. They realized that there was nothing personal in the faith that their pastor proclaimed. His preaching was little more than a history lesson with a moralizing application. The revision of his call was handled with quiet grace, but the decision was firm. It was not about an inability to tell personal stories of faith from the pulpit. It was a decision based on a belief that preaching should offer witness to faith in God and witness of the grace of God observed in the lives of people.

Autobiography offered in the pulpit, when conducted with care, has an honored place as long as it doesn't become a shortcut for interpreting the gospel. Witness to faith in God and the work of the grace of God in the lives of people about us should be present in most sermons. But as preachers we need to accept that it is gospel truth that interprets us, rather than our lives that interpret it.

THE VIRTUE OF HUMILITY

The call to be humble, to live absent of the conceits that ego constantly invites—that it is by *our* gifts and *our* talents that advantage is to be had—makes clear that hubris is the opposite of humility. Dictionaries fail us or, better, pale in depicting this virtue so eloquently explored in the Christ-poem Paul uses as his sermon text in Philippians 2:

> Let the same mind be in you that was in Christ Jesus, who, though he was in the form of God, did not regard equality with God as something to be exploited, but emptied himself, taking the form of a slave, being born in human likeness. And being found in human form, he *humbled* himself and became obedient to the point of death—even death on a cross. (Phil. 2:5-8, emphasis added)

"When Scripture tells us to discard all personal and selfish considerations," John Calvin writes of this passage, "it does not only exclude from our minds the desire for wealth, the lust for power, and the favor of others, but also banishes false ambitions and the hunger for human glory with other more secret evils. Indeed Christians ought to be disposed and prepared to keep in mind that they have to reckon with God every moment of their lives."[20] Richard Foster, a thoughtful contemporary guide of Christian spirituality, writes, "Put in simple terms humility means to live as close to truth as possible: the truth about ourselves, the truth about others, and the truth about the world in which we live."[21] To take up the virtue of humility is to adopt this other-centered rather than self-centered way of the cross. It is to live into one virtue that, apart from which, all other virtues are but mere appearance.[22]

When God is pushed to the side because some other concern dominates the preacher's heart and mind, the preacher is giving in to the vice of egoism. Ambition is not something that must be negated at all costs. Paul wrote of his ambition to teach fellow believers, to preach the gospel, and in all things to please God; but he also spoke of those who preached Christ from envy, rivalry, and selfish ambition (Phil. 1:15-17). The challenge when ego is involved is how the preacher responds to the possibilities of power that come with preaching.

Friedrich Nietzsche argued that all humans have a "will to power," a driving force to experience achievement, ambition, and approval. There is nothing wrong with this, and directed well it becomes a means to realize deep meaning in one's life. The question for preachers is what identity resources do they turn to in order to keep Christ and dependence on God central to their ambition rather than letting ambition become an end in itself.

A 1999 Higher Education Research Institute study found that 70.4% of young people choosing to go to college selected "to be well off financially" as one of the primary reasons they were pursuing higher education. That was a 31.3% raise from only 39.1% of students who chose that as a primary reason in 1970. At the same time the choice of going to college to develop a "meaningful philosophy of life" fell from 82.9% in 1967 to only 41.1% in 1999. In summarizing this radical shift in priorities among American college students, Wheaton College's Arthur Holmes suggests that it represents a radical trend in both American culture and in higher education. We are rapidly losing a value-grounding worldview as central to education, and the idea of the university has too often been seduced by the market-driven purpose of educating students for careers rather than educating them to be citizens. We are producing, he writes, students whose view of life "is best described as uncritical egoism."[23]

Should we be surprised that as participants in this radical shift in cultural perspective that American clergy can be equally seduced by the lure of material prosperity and success? Uncritical egoism comes naturally to all of us unless we purposefully challenge it by grounding our worldview in the gospel and our identity in Christ. If a preacher has grounded her or his identity in Christ, they are less apt to be led astray by the will to experience increasing power over others. The call to be humble when it comes to personal power should not be set in opposition to acclaim. Acclaim can have its benefits. Acclaim can gain an audience for the message of the gospel. What preachers must be wary of is the temptation of uncritical egoism.

Pastor John Claypool explored what the identity resources are that can help preachers remain true to their calling in his 1979 Lyman Beecher Lectures. Preachers, he argued, must work to be transparent in their own journey of faith, and out of that experience they will develop the identity resources to become:

- Reconcilers—Although the task of an orator is to mobilize people to act, the task of a preacher is to speak in ways that reestablish a relationship of trust between the human creature and the Creator.
- Gift-givers—As those who have deeply experienced this trust as the gift of God's grace and forgiveness, preachers are called to speak as gift-givers rather than as need-receivers.

- Witnesses—As those who speak out of "gift love" rather than "need love," preachers testify to their own experience of coming to terms with faith because only what has happened to them can happen through them.

- Nurturers—As those who find themselves on a journey of maturing faith in dependence on God, preachers learn to speak a word of faith to others in those moments when the other can hear what is said as Word of faith for them.

In 1985 Bob had an opportunity to talk with Claypool at a preaching conference held in Spokane, Washington. By that time Claypool had made the decision to leave the Southern Baptist pulpit in order to take up orders for the Episcopal ministry. He was already attending the Episcopal Seminary in Austin the summer they talked. Of course the question Bob had was not so much, "Why are you leaving the SBC?" but "Isn't becoming an Episcopal priest a rather dramatic alternative?"

"I am in danger," Claypool admitted, "of becoming a victim of my own acclaim in the pulpit. At this stage of my life," he confessed, "I want to do work where the mystery of the Eucharist matters more than my ability to move people from the pulpit." The national mailing list for Claypool's weekly sermons was already extensive. "I'll always love preaching," he said, "but what I need at this point in my life is the discipline of submitting my ego to serve in a tradition where the centrality of celebrating the Eucharist is the Word that speaks the witness of my faith."[24] He was ordained an Episcopal priest the following year and served for fourteen years as Rector of Saint Luke's Episcopal Church in Birmingham, Alabama, until he retired in 2000.

Humility and Autobiography

Pulpit practice must be characterized by an unselfish concern for the welfare of others and the unassuming proclamation of gospel. There is a difference between honoring clergy for their ability to witness to the power of faith versus exalting a pastor for building a personal religious empire. One need only listen to the opening words of a guest speaker in the black church tradition to see the power that comes with honoring the voice of one who has served the church well. Acclaim is offered because of the power of that pastor's pulpit rather than the personal power of his or her persuasiveness. In other words, acclaim can come to a preacher who has been considered faithful to the gospel by those who have discovered the source of the message rather than simply the magnetism of the messenger.

This is the kind of acclaim that allowed Paul to preach before Festus, and it can be the basis of how individuals in each generation give presence to a new hearing of the gospel message. The goal of authentic ethos in preaching needs to avoid making effectiveness an end, striving instead to be altruistically selfless in the proclamation of God. Egoism is a vice of self-absorption rather than faithfulness to gospel. The goal of selfless ethos in preaching needs to be faithfulness not familiarity.

This kind of acclaim can become a form of narcissism if the preacher begins to worry more about whether the next project will advance his or her reputation rather than give presence to the message of the gospel. For those who have a reputation through writing and other forms of media that transcends their local context, this is a constant question of humility; they must keep in mind that it is the message that is transforming the lives of people rather than their particular style of delivering it. For preachers whose reputation is still primarily that of the pastor of a local congregation, the struggle with unwitting narcissism is more often one of autobiographical overload. We return to this issue of narcissism in the pulpit in chapter 7.

When it comes to autobiographical illustrations in preaching, seminary professors who have read Karl Barth and Paul Tillich argue that preachers need to provide a theologically thick message in which such personal stories should have little place.[25] William Willimon almost agrees. There are times he admits when he has wanted to tell seminarians in a preaching class, "Never, under any circumstance, tell anything about yourself, or what has happened to you, done to you or by you, including anything cute done to any of your children, in a sermon!" But *never* is too strong he concludes because revealing ourselves is an essential aspect of preaching. "The Good News is meant to be embodied, inculcated, practiced, performed. Paul was right to offer himself as evidence." We need to walk a line, he suggests, between "preaching Christ and parading ourselves."[26] In the words of John Claypool we need to learn how and when to share a measure of transparency about our own journey of faith because people listen to us as one who testifies to how and why faith continues to matter.

 ## FOR FURTHER READING

Debby Applegate. *The Most Famous Man in America: A Biography of Henry Ward Beecher*. New York: Doubleday, 2006.

David Fleer and Dave Bland, eds. *Preaching Autobiography: Connecting the World of the Preacher and the World of the Text*. Abilene, TX: ACU Press, 2001.

Joel Gregory. *Too Great a Temptation: The Seductive Power of America's Super Church*. Fort Worth: Summit Group, 1994.

André Resner. *Preacher and Cross: Person and Message in Theology and Rhetoric*. Grand Rapids, MI: Eerdmans, 1999.

Barbara Brown Taylor. *Leaving Church: A Memoir of Faith*. San Francisco: Harper One, 2007.

Chapter Four

THE
ꙮ MANIPULATOR ꙮ

We begin with two stories that share in common one thing—the degree to which greediness for approval links them.

In the 1980s, Jimmy Swaggart, a pastor ordained by the Assemblies of God, led the Family Worship Center in Baton Rouge, Louisiana, a ministry that reached far beyond one church. According to Swaggart's website, at that time his television ministry reached 3,000 stations, 8 million viewers in the United States, and 500 million viewers worldwide. He was reported to have received contributions of at least $500,000 a day. But all of that changed on February 21, 1988, when Swaggart confessed to God, his congregation, and millions of viewers that he had sinned.[1]

Swaggart opened his sermon by assuring listeners he would speak from his heart and not a manuscript. "I have never sidestepped or skirted un-pleasantries. I have tried to be like a man and to preach this gospel exactly as I have seen it without fear or reservation or compromise. I can do no less this morning."[2] While he alluded to his sin, he never said what it was. Listeners discovered later that he had met with a prostitute in a motel room.

Alluding to David's sin with Bathsheba, Swaggart then began to apologize—to his wife, his son, the congregation, and his television viewers. Finally, he turned to God, "I have sinned against you, my Lord, and I would ask that Your precious blood would wash and cleanse every stain until it is in the seas of God's forgetfulness, never to be remembered against me anymore." It was at that point that Swaggart sobbed out his declaration and his apology. Swaggart's "I Have Sinned" sermon has been described as "the single most effective tele-visual performance of any American Evangelist."[3]

A compelling case can be made, however, that Swaggart's "Prize of the High Calling" comeback sermon offered only a few months after the "I Have Sinned" sermon was even more rhetorically effective.[4] In this sermon the true expression of the manipulator becomes evident. He reminded the viewing congregation that in reaching for the prize of the high calling we have in Christ, we must follow the example of Paul in "forgetting those things which are behind." He

41

acknowledged that there are many in the media who would never let him forget but that he had been directed by the Holy Spirit to do just that: forget. Otherwise he would be unable to reach the prize. And how is it possible to forget such things? The answer is to lay guilt aside, for it will only cripple a person in their ability to run the race. The answer, according to Swaggart, was to let Jesus overcome all impediments to achieving victory.

As one who had sought forgiveness and received it from his family, congregation, and God, he claimed there should be no barrier to keep him from proclaiming the gospel. He was a forgiven sinner! His having sought forgiveness should have been sufficient; or so he believed. Left unsaid was his decision to abandon his denomination's requirement of counseling before he could be permitted to return to the pulpit. Instead, Swaggart used the sermon to make the argument that his sincerity and God's forgiveness were sufficient.

Manipulators often become convinced that pious intentions and personal sincerity deserve vindication. Such preachers even manipulate their theology to justify what they want to do and then believe they are justified in their efforts to convince listeners to accept that same reasoning. We label this an unknowing manipulation because the preacher must ignore his or her own motivations to act this irresponsibly.

Next we turn to knowing manipulation and the kind of temptation too many pastors practice in their greed for approval from listeners. When it comes to knowing manipulation, preachers need to learn to "Just say No!" to "glurge" in the pulpit.

Not long after the advent of the Internet, Bob began receiving regular e-mails asking if he was "that" Rob Reid—the Rob Reid who was the original author of "that" tablecloth story. Sermon illustrations have swept the nation time and again, but the Internet makes it possible for "Chicken Soup for the Soul" stories to go viral. In this one, a minister bought a large tablecloth at an auction to cover up a hole in his church wall above the altar. A stranger found her way into his church and was shocked to see the cloth, "It was mine. My husband had it made for me before the war." She then shows the pastor her initials on the back and tells the pastor that she and her husband had been separated by the war. Her husband had been killed. Ah, but that is not the end of the story.

The pastor purchased the tablecloth to hide the hole because Christmas was coming. During the Christmas Eve service another visitor attends and approaches him about the cloth. This time it is the husband who is similarly shocked when he sees his wife's tablecloth hanging on the wall. He tells the pastor it was a gift from him to his wife who died in the war. The pastor excitedly tells him that he believes his wife is not dead. The pastor searches for, finds, and touchingly reunites the long-separated couple. Told well, there would not be a dry eye in the house.

Snopes.com, which describes and debunks urban legends, offers many variations on this popular sermon illustration. It appears to have been written by the Reverend Howard Schade who was the pastor of First Reformed Church in Nyack, New York, in the early 1950s. He subsequently published the story in *Reader's Digest* in which the "as told by Pastor Rob Reid" authentication was added. Snopes.com researched the veracity of the story and concluded it was composed whole cloth (pun intended) by Rev. Shade to tug at the heartstrings of his parishioners. What this Bob Reid came to appreciate was fifty years later, and because of the Internet, "The Gold and Ivory Tablecloth" story was still making its way into the pulpit as a true story. "Are you the Rob Reid who my pastor said told this story?" In print: no!

The people at Snopes.com label such stories *glurge*. The online Urban Dictionary says *glurge* is a syrupy sweet story sent by mass e-mails to often unwilling recipients with the added message "Pass this along 2 as many ppl as u can!!!11!!1." Snopes says glurge are overly sentimental, sickeningly sweet stories designed to bring tears to the eyes with some "uplifting moral lesson" either stated or implied. "Think of it as chicken soup," they write, "with several cups of sugar mixed in."[5]

Glurge isn't limited to stories either. A good friend of Lucy's, who also teaches homiletics, grew so tired of hearing students close sermons with the poem (we use that word loosely here) "Footprints in the Sand" that she forbade its use in her class. It was saccharine sentimentality, all sweetness and no caloric content (that is, it really is biblically and theologically unsound). One day, at the end of the school year, as she walked into the classroom building, she was met with paper-shaped footprints leading down the hall. She followed the footprints only to discover that her preaching students had commandeered a classroom and set up a "Footprints in the Sand" exhibit. The room was filled with posters, paintings, mugs, pens, jewelry, and everything imaginable that could contain the poem—all nicely merchandised for Christian consumers.

Whether we speak of preachers trying to manipulate listeners in order to justify themselves or preachers trying to manipulate the emotions of parishioners to get them to feel good about a sermon's message, greed is still the common denominator. We suspect that the sin of glurge in the pulpit is far more common than perfidy in the pulpit. Too many preachers today are tempted to reach for glurge to illustrate an idea rather than to determine whether their efforts to move listeners have integrity. In their greediness for approval of their sermonic insight, they are engaging in the equivalent of saying "Pass this along 2 as many ppl as u can!!!11!!1."

Parishioners can go to the store to buy a surge protector. But they have to trust their pastor to protect them from glurge in the pulpit. It's up to preachers to impose a glurge protector on their sermons. Ask yourself, does the story I'm thinking of using reveal an aspect of the heart of God or just tug on my listener's heartstrings?

THE MANIPULATOR AND THE PROBLEM OF GREEDINESS

Manipulate—"to handle or control," from the Latin *manus*, meaning "hand"—is an interesting word. On one hand (yes, another pun intended) it is one of the skills or abilities that make us human. We have the ability to manipulate, to use our fingers to pick up and to use tools, to play musical instruments, and to write. Several summers ago, Bob had to chase a raccoon out of his house. Bob closed a sliding pocket door to keep the critter contained only to be surprised when the coon simply reached up and slid the door to the left and raced further inside. Raccoons have an opposable thumb. They can manipulate a door as easily as a human. So, there may be raccoon moments to be accounted for in explaining the biology of manipulation, but the ability to manipulate objects is one of the wonderful abilities that characterize what it means to be human.

When it comes to speeches and preaching, however, manipulation takes on another, less-than-noble human dimension. Instead of manipulating an inanimate object, manipulating people is about controlling them or coercing their assent. The Latin word *manus*, after all, also means "force" and "violence." From antiquity we have realized that people can use communication to deceive, mislead, exploit, and oppress others. Aristotle tells us that clever communicators can take advantage of what he calls the "defects of hearers."[6] Why? Because reasoning and persuasion deal in matters of making judgments rather than proving certainties. Hearers can be swayed by making appeals to their passions or hiding relevant information from them. "Nobody," he says, "uses fine language when teaching geometry." Forming judgments is a function of human reasoning in matters in which the truth cannot be known. And human reasoning can all too easily be manipulated—especially when greedy people use "fine language" to do it.

The Problem of Greediness

Ego and passionate greed for power often combine at the expense of ethics. Rhetorically, manipulation is a crisis of failed pathos. Passion left to its own device invariably leads to greed for the approval of listeners. It creates its own appetite for more and eventually is willing to win at any cost. The greed that may be the most dangerous is that which cloaks itself in pious motives. Though many would have already counted Swaggart as one of the master manipulators of televised religion, his greed to hold on to the empire he had built had become an all-consuming passion that blinded him to responsible pulpit conduct. When someone is caught in the lie, that person usually tries to distance himself or herself from it. But if an individual who is also lying to himself is caught in that lie, he often embraces it and makes it his cause célèbre. He is engaging in unknowing greed.

Greed can also occur even when the preacher does not lie to himself. In his classic, *The Scarlet Letter*, Nathaniel Hawthorne gives us a glimpse into the mental anguish of a preacher, Arthur Dimmesdale, who not only recognized the depravity of his sin but also knew that he was manipulating his congregation by not confessing it openly. (We definitely recommend this book to you. If you remember it only as a high-school class assignment, you are missing this rich social comment.) In a chapter that Hawthorne entitled "The Interior of a Heart," we enter Dimmesdale's torment and agony. He was personally "gnawed and tortured by some black trouble of the soul." Yet through the sorrow that led him to speak, he became immensely popular with his listeners. Hawthorne writes:

> But this very burden it was, that gave him sympathies so intimate with the sinful brotherhood of mankind; so that his heart vibrated in unison with theirs, and received their pain into itself, and sent its own throb of pain through a thousand other hearts, in gushes of sad, persuasive eloquence. . . . The people knew not the power that moved them thus. They deemed the young clergyman a miracle of holiness. They fancied him the mouth-piece of Heaven's messages of wisdom, and rebuke, and love. In their eyes the very ground on which he trod was sanctified. The virgins of his church grew pale around him, victims of a passion so imbued with religious senti-ment that they imagined it to be all religion, and brought it openly, in their white bosoms, as their most acceptable sacrifice before the altar.[7]

Poor Dimmesdale. No matter what he did, his congregation loved him, and "this public veneration tortured him!" What he could not bring himself to do was to tell the truth of what he had done: to name the sin. Many a time he thought that he would finally mount the steps of his pulpit high above the congregation and declare to them, "I, your pastor, whom you so reverence and trust, am utterly a pollution and a lie!" But even when he told them that he was a vile sinner they seemed to love him all the more. And he did not disabuse them of their reaction for "he had spoken the very truth, and transformed it into the veriest falsehood. . . .Therefore, above all things else, he loathed his miserable self."

Does this sound like Rev. Swaggart? One is a knowing manipulator while the other is a pious one. We think Dimmesdale's story is more accurately an example of William Faulkner's great dictum, "The only thing worth writing about is the human heart in conflict with itself."[8] If a preacher's passion in the pulpit emerges from his or her struggle to be careful of listeners and faithful to the gospel it can be God's word. That struggle may actually be "the only thing worth preaching about"—at least insofar as it represents the preacher's effort to demonstrate respectfulness and faithfulness in his or her coming to terms with the gospel.

Marks of the Manipulator

Knowing vs. Unknowing Manipulation

Notice we have raised several kinds of manipulative behaviors in this chapter. The first is a continuum of the manipulator as a knowing sinner. On one end is the preacher who seeks to manipulate the congregation at a particular time for a particular reason. This is the person, like Swaggart, who has been caught in a lie or some difficult situation. All Christians, as Martin Luther reminded us, are *simul pecator*, "always sinners." There are moments in anyone's career, like in Swaggart's career, that may require a public apology for sin. But it is always irresponsible, whether it is sexual misconduct, financial misdealing, or some other moral lapse, for the preacher to step into the pulpit to curry favor to avoid being held accountable for these sins.

At the other end is the preacher, like Dimmesdale, who recognizes that every Sunday when he climbs into the pulpit he is manipulating his congregation. Dimmesdale's struggle was that he knew he was presenting an inauthentic self. He was not the person that his congregants thought him to be. He stood in the pulpit harboring secret sin, which he would not admit to his listeners—sin that had they known of it would have meant the end of his ministry among them.

Thinking vs. Unthinking Manipulation

A second continuum is the thinking versus unthinking practice of glurge in the pulpit. Reverend Schade belongs at one end of this continuum. He likely contrived a story (according to Snopes.com) to pull at the heartstrings of listeners in support of some long-lost sermon point. At the other end of this continuum are those who pass on glurge from chicken soup sources (true or not), the sole purpose of which is to warm the hearts of parishioners. One offers a knowing fabrication meant to move listeners while the other passes on heartwarming stories, probably true, also meant to move listeners. The problem isn't whether they are factually true or fabricated.[9] The problem is that use of such stories says more about the greediness of the preacher for approval than the worthiness of the gospel. Knowing and unknowing use of glurge are equally unworthy of listeners.

Playing to Emotions vs. Emotional Blackmail Manipulation

A third continuum has to do with being honest with ourselves when it comes to motives behind outright manipulation. At one end of this continuum the preacher constantly plays to emotions, and at the other end the preacher uses emotional blackmail. Both forms of manipulation seek to override the autonomy of listeners.

The stoic Mr. Spock in the *Star Trek* saga was convinced that the proper way to make decisions was to depend solely upon objective logic. In reality, emotion cannot be removed from judgment. It is a formative factor in the beliefs, values, and attitudes we draw on when reflecting on efforts to influence us. Studies of people who have suffered brain trauma resulting in the inability to experience any emotions, positive or negative, have demonstrated that these individuals have trouble making choices. They simply don't care. So, a crucial part of connecting with the congregation is to match the proper emotion to the nature of our appeals. In his *Institutio Oratoria,* Quintilian observed, "It is in its power over the emotions that the life and soul of oratory is to be found."[10] We have to care, and we want those to whom we are speaking to care as well. But making appeals to people's emotions does not justify playing to emotions.

There is a dramatic difference between reading Swaggart's "I Have Sinned" sermon and seeing it; Swaggart's tears are a compelling part of the nonverbal message, in many ways more persuasive than his words. Although some people may be put off by tears, many more are not able to help feeling sorry for him. We are not always able to control our emotional responses, and Swaggart sought to take advantage of the fact that he was speaking to people who cared for him and would support and protect him if they felt that he was the victim—an emotive appeal for emotive sake. Though the temptation to play to people's emotions can be great, it is irresponsible to manipulate the autonomy of listeners in this manner.

Manipulators also seek to override the autonomy of their listeners if they make use of emotional blackmail in the pulpit. We tend to recognize this "blackmail" quality more readily with interpersonal communication:

- If you really loved me . . .
- After all I have done for you . . .
- How can you be so selfish . . .[11]

Now listen to these same appeals to fear, obligation, and guilt in their sermonic equivalents as emotional blackmail from the pulpit:

- If you really loved God . . . Christ . . . the church, etc.
- After all that people before you have sacrificed . . .
- How can we be so selfish . . .

The problem with labeling this pulpit blackmail is that preachers rarely admit when some other purpose is leading them to act or speak in an immoral manner.

One of the most manipulative things Bob has ever witnessed in the pulpit occurred when he attended the funeral of a seventeen-year-old who died as a result of an automobile accident. The teenager had been an off-and-on attender of the congregation Bob served as pastor. His parents were members of a fundamentalist church across town. That pastor was chosen to officiate at the service. When it came time for him to speak he pointed to the coffin and stated:

> This young man died tragically before he took the opportunity to confess Jesus Christ as his Lord and Savior. Because of that he is burning in hell as I speak and he will burn in hell for eternity because he did not redeem the time he was given on this earth. Unless you confess Jesus Christ as your savior before you leave here today, you can be assured that you will take the seat right next to him in hell.

The gasps from those attending the funeral did not affect the parents' stoic silence. Some people present simply burst into tears. Some of us wanted to get up and leave. Some did.

Would that minister ever admit his motives were irresponsible? Unlikely. He believed what he said. He believed that the end of getting people "saved" mattered more than the shock value of his means. His evangelistic agenda trumped all. The challenge clergy face is to reject the extremes of playing to people's emotions or using emotion to blackmail them while also realizing that emotion still plays a role in forming autonomous judgments. Preachers must be honest about their motives in the pulpit.

Temptations to take advantage of the "defect of hearers" abound. Respectful pathos demands that we respond with the virtue of carefulness in the pulpit.

THE VIRTUE OF CAREFULNESS

G. Lee Ramsey Jr., in *Care-full Preaching*, explores the nature of preaching in a manner that places the emphasis on the virtue of practicing care-fullness in making persuasive appeals. He is keenly aware that preachers can be persuasive in ways that would be a surprise to them. For example, he notes the tendency of some preachers to turn the focus on themselves. If preachers have an "individualistic anthropology and personal understanding of sin and salvation,"[12] then everything flows in one direction. If they are not careful, he writes, they will model the idea that caring flows from the preacher to the congregation, or perhaps present caring as flowing from God to the preacher, and then to the person in the pew. Either way the preacher "is constantly reminding the listeners, 'I know the way,' or even, 'I am the way.'"[13]

Without being aware of it, a preacher who adopts this communicative style ends up embodying the meta-message that the preacher is actually the one who truly cares.[14] Rather than care-full preaching, Ramsey maintains this is care-less, controlling, and even manipulative preaching. It is a form of greediness on the part of the preacher. "The emotionally needy and unaware pastor," he writes, "will consume the sheep."[15]

What would care-full preaching look like? Ramsey believes that care-full preaching that takes the formative dimension of expressing the love of God seriously will seek to:

- Form communities in which members freely extend mutual care to one another. Preaching in which mutuality is fore-fronted and self-serving or abusive language is consciously avoided.[16]
- Highlight occasions in the life of the congregation that give full presence to the core image of the church as the people of God for others. This calls for intentionality of focus in lifting up stories, good and bad, of efforts to be this caring community. It does not depend on sentimentality or tear-inducing Internet tales to make this case.[17]
- Lift out of the gathered community's common life those experiences of worship, fellowship, education, and service that can be re-presented in preaching that focuses a congregation's central identity and purpose in Christ.[18]
- Reveal loving but honest portraits of what it means to come together as a care-giving community, helping the congregation be true to the joy, possibility, and struggles of the church's calling.[19]
- Employ common language, images, symbols, and stories that assist the congregation's understanding that clergy and community stand side-by-side in their care of others.[20]

Communion and mutuality communicated in this way, says Ramsey, "allows the preacher to draw the congregation toward the desired aims of the sermon" because the preacher presents himself or herself as embedded in the same world through common ties communicated in ways that require deep listening in the life of the community of faith.[21]

With Ramsey we believe that preaching should never be characterized by a one-way model of communication.[22] Whether one adopts a more traditional didactic or propositional approach, a conversational approach, or Ramsey's "care-full" approach, a preacher must always realize that unexamined assumptions embodied in the meta-message of the preaching event often speak louder than the sermon's cognitive content. The virtue of careful-ness does not occur without thoughtful attention. We are called to make sensitive use of appeals, especially emotional appeals, in preaching. Our vocation requires preachers to exercise intentional self-control in how we frame our appeals.

Portrait of a Care-full Preacher

In the summer of 2011, as we were completing our work on this book, preacher and evangelist John Stott died. He had just turned ninety. He was able to look back on a life well lived in the service of God. Stott was ordained in The Church of England and spent his whole life, as child and eventually rector, at All Souls Church in London.

Lucy attended All Souls in the mid-1990s, and, although he was retired, Rev. Stott preached that morning. Most Church of England parishes were limping along with half-empty churches, but it was standing-room-only that morning at All Souls. Even the balcony was jammed. As an evangelical in a confessional tradition that disdained evangelicals, Stott once said of himself, "An evangelical is a plain, ordinary Christian." When that plain, ordinary Christian died, newspapers around the world marked his passing.

In a reflection on the meaning of Stott's influence on evangelicalism, Mark Galli, the senior managing editor of *Christianity Today*, noted that the movement is in a time of crisis. Galli believes that evangelicalism is beset by manipulators rather than evangelists:

> For many, the disaffection [with evangelicalism] started with the rise of our movement's two crazy uncles, Pat Robertson and Jerry Falwell. . . . Add to that the televangelist scandals (Bakker and Swaggart, in particular), the flooding of the Christian marketplace with Christian kitsch . . . and the crass self-promotion of evangelical mega-pastors and mega-authors—well, it made the ordinary and thoughtful evangelical wonder if something is wrong at the core of the movement.[23]

Galli finds hope when looking across the life, the ministry, the preaching, and the example of John Stott. If one were to reread the works of Stott, one would find sermons "that were true and faithful to the text of the Bible." He did not "overwhelm the biblical narrative with his own cute stories." And there was no "pandering after the crowds" (which we will explore in the next chapter). In Stott's preaching there was "no studied attempt to be authentic, no pacing up and down the stage, no working the crowd for a laugh. Just simple and clear exegesis, with the appropriate illustration or classic quote."[24]

For Galli, John Stott represents a portrait of the care-full preacher who has served Christ responsibly in the pulpit. He was a model of self-control, a man who:

- lived a life that was true and faithful to the Bible
- spoke with conviction and humility
- worked hard and played hard, but did not burn out
- listened to his critics without being cowed by them
- wore fame lightly
- continued to grow and learn his whole life
- expanded on God's calling on his life until his last breath
- put love into action

Would that such an epitaph could be offered for all who would preach the gospel. God calls all to the virtue of being care-full preachers.

FOR FURTHER READING

Mark Galli. "John Stott and the Weary Evangelical: What the Movement Looks Like at its Best." *Christianity Today*. http://www.christianitytoday.com/ct/2011/augustweb-only/johnstottwearyevangelical.html.

Michael J. Giuliano. *Thrice Born: The Rhetorical Comeback of Jimmy Swaggart.* Macon, Ga.: Mercer Press, 1999.

Henry H. Mitchell. *Celebration and Experience in Preaching*. Nashville: Abingdon Press, 1990.

G. Lee Ramsey Jr. *Care-full Preaching: From Sermon to Caring Community*. St. Louis: Chalice Press, 2000.

Chapter Five

THE
ஜ PANDERER ௸

In 1992, during a primary debate, presidential candidate Bill Clinton said that he would support the development of a new submarine program, the Seawolf. Soon after that remark one of Clinton's opponents, Paul Tsongas, a former senator from Massachusetts, lashed out at his fellow Democrat, claiming that Clinton's stance was made purely as a way to get votes. Clinton, he argued, knew that the program would never go forward. He claimed that Clinton voiced his support simply as an appeal to voters in Connecticut where those submarines were to have been built. Tsongas wanted the American public to know how "cynical and unprincipled" Clinton was. He declared that Clinton was a just a "pander bear . . . who will say anything, do anything to get votes."[1]

Clinton went on to win the election and become the forty-second president, but Tsongas's label stuck. And it stuck, not only to Clinton, but to many candidates. Tsongas had introduced a new and lasting epithet into the political vocabulary. Since the 1992 campaign, both Democratic and Republican candidates have been accused of being pander bears.

A panderer, as Tsongas pointed out, is one who says anything, promises anything, and does anything in order to win votes or approval or to please people. Although no relation to a panda bear, the original panderer was Pandarus, a figure in Greek mythology. He appears in the *Iliad* as an impetuous Lycian who fought for the Trojans and ultimately brokered a truce with the Greeks by shooting Menelaus. Authors such as Chaucer and Shakespeare eventually transformed the archetype of a panderer to a character who plays the go-between for ill-fated lovers.

Former congressman Paul Simon provides us with a contemporary assessment of the problem of pandering:

> We have spawned "leadership" that does not lead, that panders to our whims rather than telling us the truth, that follows the crowd rather than challenging us, that weakens us rather than strengthening us. It is easy to go downhill, and we are now following the easy

path. Pandering is not illegal, but it is immoral. It is doing the convenient when the right course demands inconvenience and courage. Leaders in all areas—including politics, media, religion, and education—are guilty of pandering, of giving in to what is easy instead of fighting for what is right.[2]

Pandering and the character of the panderer have come to be identified with those who satisfy people's basest desires or weaknesses.

In the previous chapter we explored the sin of manipulation in the pulpit when preachers disrespect their listeners by manipulating emotional appeals. In this chapter we argue that the panderer manipulates and rejects the gospel message in order to win the adulation and adoration of the people in the pews. So what does a preaching pander bear look like? What does she do? What does he say?

THE PANDERER AND THE PROBLEM OF TRENDINESS

Lucy began to get a sense of the depth of the addiction to pandering in the pulpit some years ago when she gave a talk at the Festival of Homiletics. Recognizing the importance of illustrations and stories in sermons, she encouraged and challenged the preachers before her to name God, through Scripture, in their own lives and the lives of their congregants rather than to depend on the thousands of sermon stories and illustrations available in books and now on the Internet. She argued that parishioners would rather sit down to a home-cooked meal instead of preaching's equivalent to Hamburger Helper. Stories are more than mere filler, entertainment, or attention getters; stories are theology. They are often the strongest takeaway from a sermon. They are the resources we provide to help people discover what God is doing here and now.

Lucy called for careful reading of Scripture; attention to the news, television, and movies; and listening to the joys, sorrows, and questions of surrounding people as a means to provide preachers with what Jennifer Lord describes as "resurrection speech." Resurrection speech, according to Professor Lord, depicts preaching with integrity and gives voice "to the power of death and God's power of new life in our midst."[3] If we are to offer resurrection speech in the pulpit, Lord says preachers must learn to pay close attention to the events occurring in local and global contexts in order to make the vital connections between the world of the biblical texts and the world of living Christianly as people of the resurrection in our time.

Building on this insight from Professor Lord, Lucy told the festival attendees that she can always tell when a seminary student begins to read a story in a sermon pulled from the Internet or from a liturgical resource. Voice, facial expression, and even body language all change and the student becomes a narrator rather than a preacher. Borrowed stories don't have the same gravitas as those we develop from our own listening and our own reflection on what is happening in the contexts we pay close attention to. That doesn't mean that as a preacher you can't tell a story of a historical figure or a powerful story that truly illuminates. But a power shortage occurs when we start to look for illustrations from others rather than offer "resurrection speech" in the pulpit. Give up your addiction to canned chicken soup, she encouraged, and begin making your own homemade nourishing broth.

After the talk a number of people came to speak with her. One person excitedly told her that he had already come to that same conclusion. He had thrown away bookshelves filled with sermon-illustration books and found it very freeing. He also witnessed that his congregation had responded to the change. As the group surrounding Lucy shared their responses to her challenge, a man stood off to the side, clearly waiting for everyone to leave. Finally, he could not wait any longer. He broke into the circle and confronted Lucy, "I hated everything you said." With that he turned on his heel and left. Lucy had no opportunity to ask him what he hated and why. He was gone. But she was left to assume that he was unwilling, or unable, to give up his addiction to canned soup.[4]

The Temptation of Trendiness

Marsha Witten may well have identified one of the most serious crises that can arise from a failed theology of responsible persuasive preaching. She provides an in-depth analysis of forty-seven Presbyterian and Southern Baptist sermons on Luke 15:11-32, the parable of the prodigal [and elder] son. Among her findings about the three primary ways this text is treated in the preaching she surveys (e.g., accommodation, resistance, and reframing), accommodation represents the most worrisome element for her. She found that, in their need to accommodate the language of the sermon to the interests and relevance of their listeners, the preachers surveyed had a strong tendency to downplay important aspects of Christian belief and accommodate it to popular interests. What she found was substance giving way to trendiness. She asks:

> What . . . of the immensely potent Protestant doctrine of grace which appears eviscerated in much of the speech as speakers fail to acknowledge notions of human depravity and separation from a transcendent God? What of the ability of religious speech to deal with concerns of theodicy, if it declines to contend with issues of human suffering and evil? What of the possibilities for creating and sustaining stable, binding communities of faith, if incentives to congregation are based purely on mutable perceptions of self-interest?[5]

It is a path of least resistance to become a pander bear with our theological substance as well as our use of stories. Are we settling for correction speech rather than taking up the challenge to embrace resurrection speech? If we ask, "How did we come to this?" the answer must include a recognition that the muscle exercised in the name of a theology of persuasive preaching too often can be weakened by our desire to be trendy, insightful, and just plain popular.

Bring Us Your Rich and Your Needy

The American experiment in democracy also generated experiments in preaching and worship. At the dawn of the nineteenth century, people began the push to open the new nation's frontiers, and with that came the development of camp meetings and revivals. We also saw the rise of the preacher as entertainer. Henry Ward Beecher was so popular that the boats that ferried people by the thousands from Manhattan to his church in Brooklyn on Sunday morning were known as Beecher boats.

In the age of P. T. Barnum, preachers had to compete, and one of those showman preachers was Billy Sunday. (Billy's birth name was actually that, William Ashley Sunday.) Raised in Iowa, Sunday began his career as a professional baseball player, but a conversion experience in Chicago led him to leave baseball and turn to the ministry. After many years of assisting an evangelist in the Midwest, Sunday began his own crusades. Although the preacher under whom he had studied was urbane and sophisticated, Billy Sunday became known for his folksy, energetic, and very dramatic sermons. He did anything to draw people to his revivals.

Early in his preaching career he advertised his revivals by staging baseball games. Wearing his old uniform, Sunday played for each team. He also employed a circus giant as an usher. But soon those publicity stunts were no longer needed, and he was preaching in tents and eventually wooden "tabernacles" that held almost twenty thousand people. Because the buildings were so large the floors were covered with sawdust to muffle the sound. Many argued his revivals were more like circuses than worship.

But the enormously popular preachers of the nineteenth and early twentieth centuries such as Beecher, Sunday, and Charles Grandison Finney eventually gave way to the next generation. The middle of the twentieth century saw the rise of another Billy—Billy Graham—who was forced to rent sports stadiums as the only venues large enough to fit the crowds that would gather every night for a week in the city where a crusade was held. Robert Schuller replaced the sawdust and timbered tabernacle, first with an old drive-in movie theater and then with a gleaming cathedral of crystal. They were the forerunners of today's entertaining preachers such as the Reverend Joel Osteen, who has combined these approaches, housing a congregation in a former indoor sports arena in Houston, Texas, to meet the worship needs of 43,500 people a week. At this writing this is the largest congregation in the United States, but we suspect that with the rapid growth of simulcast preaching on any number of screens, pastors who meet the needs of congregations simultaneously in multiple states will probably claim even larger numbers in the very near future. A twist on the latter is the growing trend of congregations that offer multiple venues for worship, "each with a different worship style, but all with the same simulcast message delivered by our senior pastor."

Exciting ImMEDIAte Passions and Other Dangerous Nonsense

We shouldn't be surprised by preachers who blur the line between preaching and entertainment. It's easy to preach to people's passions. In his now classic *Amusing Ourselves to Death*, Neil Postman argued that "the mediums of communication available to a culture are a dominant influence on the formation of the culture's intellectual and social preoccupations." Over a decade before the advent of the Internet, before iPhones and iPads, Postman made the prophetic observation that people of our generation are experiencing "a vast and trembling shift from the magic of writing to the magic of electronics."[6] And Postman hadn't even imagined texting and tweeting!

Charles Finney did not want his revivals to be boring. And Billy Sunday was never accused of being dull. After taking a great deal of time to view televangelists such as Robert Schuller, Oral Roberts, Jimmy Swaggart, Jerry Falwell, Jim Bakker, and Pat Robertson, Postman realized two things:

> He only needed to watch about five hours of these televised holy men to realize everything that "makes religion an historic, profound and sacred human activity is stripped away; there is no ritual, no dogma, no tradition, no theology, and above all, no sense of spiritual transcendence . . . the preacher is tops. God comes out as second banana." A media culture, he argued, invariably reduces religion to entertainment.[7]

After noting that the electronic preachers he saw simply could not compare with the educated and theologically sophisticated evangelists of previous generations, he concluded that it was not so much their lack of education but the fact that it was the weakness of the television media that turned their preaching into pandering. On March 27, 1998, Neil Postman spoke at a conference for clergy urging them that "we need to proceed with our eyes wide open so that we may use technology rather than be used by it."[8]

We are aware that Postman represents a cautionary voice when it comes to the use of media. Does this mean that all use of media for broadcast-era preaching or in digital-era preaching should be viewed suspiciously as pandering? Hardly. In his insightful study, *The Millenium Matrix*, Rex Miller reminds us that the shift from the oral to the print cultures established the written word as the ultimate standard of authority in the church, and as a result the "focus of the [worship] service shifted from the Eucharist to the preaching of the word" in many congregations.[9] As we now transition from the broadcast era (televised preaching) to the digital era (using media in worship), we can only wonder what effect this will have for preaching.

Wise use of stimulating graphics and video clips that invite the listener to explore the texture of the world of ideas presented in a sermon can be a marvelous enhancement of preaching well when done well. Or they can be examples of technology gone astray. We who teach in classrooms know that occasionally students stay home sick from PowerPoint poisoning.

David Randolph, one of the founders of the New Homiletic, recently published a revised edition of his 1969 book, *The Renewal of Preaching*, this time calling for the Next Homiletic—a homiletic that takes seriously the implications of the digital revolution. Bob was invited to write a "Concluding Commentary" for this volume, and David took up part of his summary in the Preface stating:

> The Next Homiletics will combine Deep Faith and High Tech to deepen devotion to God and widen service to humanity. Whether the Next Homiletics will be "Digital or Dialogical" as Robert Reid puts it in his commentary, is a major question. I propose a renewal of preaching that is both dialogical and digital.[10]

David is right; *and* is generally a wise alternative to *or*. We are in David's debt once again as we try to imagine ourselves into this Next era of preaching. If engaged thoughtfully, we may even bypass some of the problems that arose with the broadcast era's embrace that too readily tried to give people what they wanted without always asking whether it was gospel.

Giving Them What They Want

So Postman's analysis of the broadcast era of communication still applies at least in raising caution concerning the digital era. Pandering is still pandering. He notes that, in the mid-1980s, the director of the National Religious Broadcasters made a point of explaining to leaders of the religious media that "you can get your share of the audience only by offering people something they want."[11] It was, of course, a direct invitation for them to pander. And pander they did.

In 2007, Senator Chuck Grassley, the ranking member of the Committee on Finance, asked six media-based ministries for information regarding their expenses, their executive compensation, and the amenities given to their executives.[12] Grassley was intent on making sure that the tax-exempt media ministries of Randy and Paula White, Benny Hinn, Joyce Meyer, Bishop Eddie Long, Creflo Dollar, and Kenneth Copeland became accountable to their donors. The individual letters directed to each of these ministries, viewable on the congressman's website, provide a laundry list of massive greed and financial abuse by these people and their religious organizations. In 2011, Grassley concluded his investigation, noting that the Joyce Meyer and Benny Hinn ministries had taken clear steps to reform unacceptable practices. The report adds, however, that,

> Four ministries either did not provide any information or provided incomplete information. Randy and Paula White of Without Walls International Church, Eddie Long of New Birth Missionary Baptist Church/Eddie L. Long Ministries, and Kenneth and Gloria Copeland of Kenneth Copeland Ministries submitted incomplete responses. Creflo and Taffi Dollar of World Changers Church International/ Creflo Dollar Ministries declined to provide any of the requested information. Findings regarding those organizations are summarized in the staff review.[13]

Are we surprised when well-packaged pandering turns into massive corruption among those from whom great honesty is expected? This is passion in the name of God gone deeply astray. We are glad that Meyer and Hinn have sought to become more responsible, but an argument can be made that their problems actually arose because they made "offering people what they want" the measure of their effectiveness rather than faithfulness to the gospel.

Does offering people what they want today mean foreswearing that old-time religion? According to an emergent pastor, the next urban generation "won't be attracted by flashy worship bands or famous preachers. . . . They want honest expression through art or conversation."[14] And according to Pastor Nadia Bolz-Weber of House for All Sinners and Saints, what they want is "anti-excellence, pro-participation" ministry.[15] We need to do better at the outset of the digital era in asking how to engage the possibilities of this digital revolution responsibly as a means to further the concerns of the gospel from the pulpit. In *Digital Storytellers*, Len Wilson contends:

> The Screen is not the best place for facts; its function is not to illustrate factual truths. The screen's function in digital age worship is to approach emotional truth. This emotive power is different from emotionalism, which is an enthusiastic state of fervor that some religious persons expect during intimacy with God. Emotive perception is a different way of encountering God . . . through the heart, and especially within the soul (rather than just the mind). This heart-and-soul communion with God occurs primarily in stories.[16]

What should be clear after a half century or more of broadcast-era preaching, during which pandering too often became a norm, is that preaching must increasingly take responsibility to see itself as part of the whole story explored in worship. The question contemporary preachers face is how to make productive use of new media as a vital resource in communicating the gospel truth to heart, soul, and mind while resisting the temptation to use these immersive mediums as a way to give persuasive presence to something that is less than or other than gospel.[17]

Will Willimon tells us that the gifted southern writer Flannery O'Connor once scoffed at a pastor she knew who, in her words, had become "one part minister and three parts masseuse" in his effort to meet all the needs of his parishioners. Willimon adds, "The gospel is not simply about meeting people's needs. The gospel is also a critique of our needs, an attempt to give us needs worth having."[18] If we make success at meeting those needs with sermons the end, then the gospel is reduced to being a means to achieving this end through preaching. However success and its measure of effectiveness get defined, when "offering people what they want" becomes the starting point that grounds a sermon's purpose, then the distinctiveness of the Christian message will be lost. Sermons that begin with this foundation may make use of Christian principles and draw on Christian affirmations, but their goal is something other than announcing good news.

Common Interests or Common Obligations?

In her book *Broken Tablets*, Rabbi Rachel Mikva writes, "A basic document for Jews, the Talmud, says that a person 'is known by his pocket, his cup and his rage.'"[19] The challenge with pandering in the pulpit is that it assumes Christians should be known by what they want and what they need rather than how the gospel transforms those wants and needs. Rabbi Mikva believes that religious communities of every kind are at their best when they are united by common obligations rather than common interests.

The temptation to entertain instead of providing substance is a temptation not only for the media minister. Every pastor is keenly aware of the constant temptation to increase the numbers of the church by trying to appeal to common interests. Of course, focusing on common interests may bring in more people, while focusing on common obligations can be off-putting to these same people. Too often people arrive at churches expecting a congregation to be like a fast-food franchise designed to meet their immediate needs—now. But an extensive 2003 report produced by the Hartford Institute for Religion Research found that congregations that "enact their faith without explicit expectations for members experience less vitality and more conflict."[20]

Paul Simon believes that clergy are particularly tempted to cater to a culture of indifference to the obligations of faith. He says, "The culture in which we live can smother the possibility of asking ourselves penetrating questions. The religious routine—or perhaps more accurately the irreligious routine—lets the pastor or priest or rabbi or imam pander to the members of his or her flock who live in comfort, ignoring the needs of those whom their faith suggests we should aid."[21] Simon argues that the greatest sin by faith leaders has been and still is "an unwillingness to do the unpopular; a tendency to comfort and pander to those who attend religious functions regularly but not disturb them by building bridges to other faiths or by helping the most miserable in our society and our world in concrete ways."[22]

What would a willingness to speak the unpopular in a pulpit entail? Simon suggests that it is "intolerable" for clergy to ignore the very real needs of people in their communities and in the world. Writing in 2003, he used the fact that 43 million Americans have no health insurance as exactly the kind of issue churches need to hear about in sermons. He is impatient with sermons that are directed only to individual needs, personal faith, and family security. What of the biblical call to care for the needs of others? Of course the preacher should not take partisan sides. But avoiding partisanship should never be used as an excuse for avoiding pressing issues. "A sermon that includes references to the issue," he writes, "needs follow-through. The difficulty in most faith groups is that we do not even get to phase one, having a sermon on the subject. Leaders are afraid it might offend someone. It might, but usually it will not, if handled properly."[23]

How can we face our common obligations to be involved in the lives of others for good? Simon suggests several ways that preachers can raise the issue and follow through with it in the life of the congregation. Following through would include such actions as:

- Inviting key members to contact religiously affiliated agencies for insight on how to get involved in making a difference in a social issue.

- Appointing a nonpartisan individual in the congregation to help direct the energies of people who wish to become more involved as an expression of their faith.

- Invite men's and women's groups in the church to be involved in assisting congregants in becoming involved in effecting political change through volunteering, in hosting debates by politicians and others in the community vested in making a difference in the matter.

- Urging parishioners to express thoughtful concern in newspaper letters to the editor and to their elected officials.[24]

Simon's council is sage advice for pastors who wish to examine their own sermons to see just how often they address the wants and needs of individualistic faith rather than the commitments and care of a generous faith. As the University of Chicago's revered historian of religion, Martin Marty, once observed, "Unless religious impulses find a home in more than the individual heart or soul, they will have few long-lasting public consequences."[25]

The problem of pandering, like the problem of greed, is still a problem of pathos gone awry, but it is often more subtle. Like many of these ethical problems, it begins with good intentions. The original goal is to make the gospel meaningful or relevant, but this too often can slide into a well-meaning result of making the gospel palatable for listeners. It is too easy to become a pander bear content to offer up pulpit soporifics of correction speech rather than take up the challenge to preach stories that embody the power of resurrection speech. It is tempting to use the pulpit to recruit people to the church based on their wants and needs rather than let the gospel critique those wants and needs. It is equally easy to pander to common interests rather than preach about common obligations. Faithful pathos that takes seriously the call to be passionate about what God is passionate about calls us to be honest with God and honest with those to whom we are called to be a witness to the grace and mercy of God.

THE VIRTUE OF HONESTY

Too many preachers today are like the disciples, seeking to fulfill human needs and wants with the wrong kind of food. When do we, as preachers, step over the line from appropriate theological questioning and into pandering? When do we replace appropriate worship with showmanship and show business? How do we know if we are stepping over the line in an effort to make the gospel palatable and easy to swallow so that we will be popular, accepted, and admired? We only need to turn to the Scriptures to discover that the followers of Jesus have been asking these questions since the beginning.

In all four Gospels, stories are told of Jesus feeding huge crowds. In each story the crowds have been following Jesus to hear his teaching and to bring their sick for healing. Finding themselves in deserted places with hungry crowds on their hands, the disciples begin to panic. What will they do if the crowd becomes a mob demanding not only healing but also food? The disciples urge Jesus to send the people away before that happens. But not only does Jesus refuse to send the people away, he also charges the disciples to feed them: "They need not go away; you give them something to eat" (Matt. 14:16). He responds to their needs. Yet, in John's Gospel, the day after Jesus feeds the crowd, the people look for Jesus. Jesus responds, "Very truly, I tell you, you are looking for me, not because you saw signs, but because you ate your fill of the loaves" (John 6:26). Jesus urges his disciples and the crowds to "not work for the food that perishes, but for the food that endures for eternal life, which the Son of Man will give you" (John 6:27).

We can definitely appreciate the disciples' concern. The people that covered the hillside needed food and water. And the followers of Christ are called to meet those real, physical needs. When, at the end of Matthew's Gospel, Jesus speaks of food and water, he is not speaking metaphorically. Jesus is talking about real bread and a cup of cool water (Matt. 25:31-46). The challenge, therefore, is to decide when do people need water that will quench their thirst and when do they need Jesus, the living water?

Doing Theology in the Pulpit

Stories, images, language choice, and delivery are all essential to the preaching event. It may be as simple as deciding in what language you will speak. Speaking in English to a gathering of individuals who understand only Spanish is the equivalent of offering them an empty cup, and over-the-top emotional displays are the equivalent of offering moldy bread. Therefore, as preachers we need checks and balances that will help us maintain our faithfulness to the gospel.

The last several decades saw an emphasis on narrative and issues of form in homiletics. What came to be identified as the "New Homiletic" helped preachers understand that, in addition to content, exegesis, and doctrine, they also needed to attend to the way that their sermon was arrayed and presented to their listeners. When Augustine sought to improve the preaching of his clergy he reminded them that their preaching needed to be balanced between teaching, moving, and delighting. Likewise, the proponents of the "New Homiletic" felt that preaching had focused too much on teaching, the propositional, and the exegetical. They sought to shift the balance more toward delight. But by a turn toward "delight" they did not mean entertainment as much as a turn toward the narrative and the experiential.

Unfortunately, pendulums do have a tendency to swing too much to one side. In the turn to delight, many would argue that balance was lost again. More recently there has been a renewed call to recover the teaching dimension of preaching. An early challenge in this movement came from Clark Williamson and Ronald Allen in their book, *The Teaching Minister*. The people of the church, they observed, have lost the ability to think theologically, to engage the questions and debates confronting the church through theological arguments. Helping people learn how to think theologically, they argue, helps them not only listen to and understand sermons, but also ultimately to live out their Christian faith.[26]

Whereas entertainment and, by extension, pandering focus on the here and now, on the ephemeral and often trivial theology and teaching, Williamson and Allen call for teaching and preaching that helps "the congregation name the world in the terms of the gospel . . . the news that God loves each and every created thing and that this love calls for justice for each and every created thing."[27] Although they offer their reader fifteen characteristics of the teaching sermon, permit us to select a few. The teaching sermon helps listeners:

- remember—or learn—the content of the gospel
- reflect critically on the situation of the community
- interpret the significance of the gospel (and the tradition) for the contemporary community

The content of the teaching sermon is:

- appropriate to the gospel
- morally credible

And the teaching preacher respects the freedom of the listeners to say *no!* to the sermon.[28]

James Kay also challenges preachers to make the theological turn. In *Preaching and Theology*, he recognizes that many preachers consider *theology* a negative word. We agree. In her introductory preaching course, Lucy does not have any difficulty helping her students understand that, as preachers, they are also biblical scholars. However, since her students put off their systematic theology coursework until the last possible moment, she has a great deal more difficulty helping them understand that as preachers they are, indeed, theologians. Kay observes, "thinking critically and theologically is necessary for preaching to proceed with honesty, integrity, and faithfulness to the Christian message."[29]

Honest to God

Practicing the virtue of honesty requires that preachers be willing to balance the same challenge that Augustine sought for preachers in his day as well. We need to be honest to God first in our calling but also find ways to invite listeners to discover the power of the gospel in their lives. We are called to share a gospel that is both good news and a critique of what a culture may propose as its version of good news. In an affluent culture in which it is easy to make many things false idols, preachers must learn to be honest with people about the good news of the gospel. We must be willing to think critically and speak theologically to the people whom God has placed in the care of our ministries. We must tell the stories of gospel truth from the biblical text and out of our reading of the culture and the lives of people about us if we desire to see our preaching become resurrection speech.

In an afterword to a recent collection of his novellas called *Full Dark, No Stars*, Stephen King asserts something about the power of stories that should challenge those of us who preach. He writes:

I have little patience with writers who *don't* take the job seriously, and none at all with those who see the art of story-telling as essentially worn out. It's not worn out, and it's not a literary game. It's one of the vital ways in which we make sense of our lives, and the often terrible world we see around us. It's the way we answer the question, *How can such things be?* Stories suggest that sometime— not always, but sometimes—there's a *reason*.[30]

In a world that increasingly asks questions of meaning, especially as we see terrible things about us, King claims that stories are essential to how we make sense of what matters. We agree. The difference is that preachers are called to find the stories that name God and name grace for people who ask, How can such things be? In preaching, it is the power of stories and the substance of theology that give preaching the ability to tell a counterstory to the way our culture offers meaning.

Story tells us who we are and who we can be. At its best, preaching presents the story of Jesus as unfinished, as awaiting final eschatological resolution. Honest preaching is intended to call people "in Christ" to live in community with others with whom they share common obligations and not just common interests. Honest preaching is intended to invite people "in Christ" to learn to actively participate in bringing to fruition this Christ story by learning to do justice, love kindness, and walk humbly before their God (Mic. 6:8). If parishioners are to comprehend what it means to be "in Christ," it will require preachers willing to be honest to God and honest with the people to whom God has called them to preach.

 FOR FURTHER READING

Stanley Hauerwas. *A Cross-Shattered Church: Reclaiming the Theological Heart of Preaching.* Grand Rapids, MI: Brazos Press, 2009.

Christine M. Smith. *Preaching as Weeping, Confession, and Resistance: Radical Responses to Radical Evil.* Louisville, KY: Westminster John Knox Press, 1992.

Len Wilson and Jason Moore. *Digital Storytellers: The Art of Communicating the Gospel in Worship.* Nashville: Abingdon Press, 2002.

Paul Scott Wilson. *Broken Words: Reflections on the Craft of Preaching.* Nashville: Abingdon Press, 2004.

Chapter   Six

THE
❧ DEMAGOGUE ❧

Any list of twentieth-century American demagogues probably includes Father Charles Coughlin, a Roman Catholic priest who became a right-wing polemicist with a radio listening audience that at the height of his fame in 1930–36 reached an estimated 35 to 40 million listeners. Pause on that number a moment: 35 to 40 million listeners. It means that almost one third of the nation's population at the time tuned in to hear this preacher every week. It means that Coughlin had the largest radio audience of any speaker in American history.

Though obscure to many today, this Catholic priest initially began broadcasting his sermons through the then-new medium of radio in 1926. Why? Because the weekly $50 gathered in the offering plate did not meet his $100 parish loan obligation. At first his sermons were biblical and devotional, but after the market crash of 1929, his talks drew more on populist politics than pastoral piety. Catholic, Protestant, Jew, and nonreligious listeners began to gather about their radios to hear his Sunday afternoon broadcast each week. Before long he could be heard on stations throughout the nation. Businesses paused so people could tune in. You could walk down the streets in neighborhoods all over America and from the open windows not miss a word of his broadcast.[1] And after each message people spent the next hour or more talking about the issues he raised. His talks mobilized the nation. His talks gave Depression-era listeners hope.

He told them who our national heroes were and who the villains were, too. He didn't hesitate to point his finger at who to blame for the nation's economic ills: "If the promoter and financier and industrialist believed in the doctrines of Jesus Christ, he would no more exploit his fellow man than he would sell the Master for thirty pieces of silver."[2] Wall Street profiteers were responsible for the plight of the common American: "Oh rob, steal, exploit and break your fellow citizens," he said giving voice to growing American anger. "Every time you lift a lash of oppression you are lashing Christ!"[3]

Coughlin soon mixed religion, politics, and patriotism. After he supported a losing candidate in the 1936 election, he sought to regain his power base by placing increasing blame for the economic ruin average people experienced on Jewish bankers and communistic conspiracies concocted by international Jewish financiers. Radio stations began to drop his weekly program, and the government eventually silenced both his radio pulpits and his right to send "propaganda" through the mail. Even after the American declaration of war in 1941, Coughlin's sermons were still filled with anti-Semitic demagoguery, alleging that the war itself was a Jewish-communistic plot, the intent of which was "the liquidation of Americanism at home."[4] By May of 1942 the newly appointed Archbishop of Detroit ordered Coughlin to cease expressing his political views in the media and limit his work to parish responsibilities.

Though his political commentary went far beyond the separation of the church and state threshold we expect in our era, it is not the politicized nature of his speech, in and of itself, that leads historians to label Coughlin as a demagogue. It was his ill-advised anti-Semitism that makes this judgment almost universal today. For our purposes, however, it is more important to grasp that the seeds of his demagogic pulpit practice were already present in the years of his immense popularity, when he received more mail each week—most of which provided both financial and vocal support of his pulpit ministry—than any other person in the nation.

So what marks his preaching as demagogic? First, he cast a wide-ranging conspiracy in which international bankers, industrialists, the government, the press, and eventually Roosevelt himself were the villains responsible for the financial ruin of the Depression and the depravation experienced by so many. Second, his heroes were the average American farmer and laborer, the nation's forefathers who imagined what once was and could be again, God and Jesus who call for social justice against the wicked, and eventually Coughlin himself. Third, he offered an eloquent closed system of reasoning, providing listeners an argument that was impervious to disproof because it employed ad hominem attacks on people rather than debate about their positions. He manipulated existing stereotypes and insecurities already held by listeners. Fourth, his platform was built on giving people scapegoats on whom to hang all their fears and frustrations. His weekly messages identified why people were suffering, who was to blame for it, and how to fix our national problems so that all Americans could enjoy prosperity.[5]

By any gauge Coughlin's populist influence during the 1930s was enormous, and his fall was barely noticed as the nation turned its attention to waging war. However, there is a counternarrative to casting Coughlin as a mere demagogue. Daniel Berrigan, the Jesuit priest who became the focal antiwar protest leader during the Vietnam War, well remembers gathering with his family to listen to Coughlin's radio messages every week in the 1930s. He recalls how Coughlin's message touched the "raw nerve" of people's experience and seemed to give a "voice to the voiceless" who were struggling with poverty and a sense of powerlessness.[6] Berrigan expresses gratitude that other

Catholic thinkers helped him rise above this kind of "hate-mongering," but he never forgot how this one priest could challenge the powers that be. And it is in just this kind of memory that we find the dilemma of what it means to be considered a demagogue. Is one person's demagogue simply another person's advocate? Is *demagoguery* just a term freely used by one group to denigrate effective leaders who advance different political positions? Is it just a synonym for what many consider engaging in hate speech? For rallying what to someone else is unpopular speech? Is there any criterion we can point to that makes someone guilty of pulpit demagoguery?

THE DEMAGOGUE AND THE PROBLEM OF EXPLOITATION

Etymologically the word *demagogue* is derived from combining two Greek words: *demos*, the word for "people," and *agogos*, the word for "leading, directing, or inciting." So the word *demagogue* was used to describe those whose oratorical skills made them particularly effective in leading or inciting people. It was a skill originally attributed to an orator who could frame appeals with great effectiveness. In modern English we use the word to describe people with a public platform who inflame popular prejudices with false claims and promises in order to increase their own power or privilege their own policies. Demagogues wield power by scapegoating or marginalizing the ideas of others in order to increase their own reputation. Politicians and pundits freely use the term as an ad hominem attack meant to undermine the political platforms of people they oppose. The irony, of course, is that the person making the claim is more likely to be the demagogue than the person being accused.

It is possible to be a demagogue without great skill as an orator. For example, Joseph McCarthy was a capable speaker but was not considered a particularly apt orator. Yet from 1950 to 1955, he wielded great power in the U.S. Senate by employing what have since been called "smear tactics" to incite the fears of Americans that communists (an out-group) had secretly infiltrated significant positions of social influence in America (the in-group) in order to overthrow cherished democratic freedoms. It eventually became apparent to most people that in the name of protecting freedom, McCarthy was wielding power as a partisan weapon against people he believed to be socialists and liberals, demagogically scapegoating anyone who questioned his political vision of appropriate American beliefs. It was his positional power rather than his oratory that puts him on the list of the great demagogues of the twentieth century.[7]

A recent communication scholar has proposed that demagoguery should be understood as the use of polarizing propaganda in which a person creates in- and out-groups with promises to listeners that by scapegoating the out-group they can return to some idealized vision of cultural stability—an emotive appeal based on what Erich Fromm famously called "an escape from freedom."[8] *Escape from Freedom* is the title of Fromm's best-known work that focuses on the normal human urge to return to the security of an idealized, ordered world of authority and certainty rather than deal with the ambiguities and uncertainties that come with the freedom of modern political democracies. There is a potential in all people, Fromm argued, to want to "escape from this kind of freedom into submission or some kind of relationship to man and the world which promises relief from uncertainty, even if it deprives the individual of his freedom."[9] And it is this desire to escape from the demands of freedom that can make the appeals of a demagogue so enticing.

Another communication scholar has summarized seven rhetorical techniques typically employed by demagogues in their efforts to scapegoat the views and people they oppose:

- personalized appeal
- oversimplification
- appeals to emotion to the exclusion of rational thought
- specious or deliberately distorted argumentation
- ad hominen attacks
- anti-intellectualism
- political pageantry[10]

The challenge with such lists is that even the best leaders can be charged with using such persuasive techniques on occasion. An elitist can be equally guilty as an emotivist in making these kinds of appeals; a noble speaker can be just as guilty as the demagogue. Thus, for our purposes a demagogue is someone who habitually uses these kinds of techniques, appealing to popular fears by promoting a dogmatically closed system of beliefs while consistently denouncing some out-group as the ones responsible for keeping listeners from realizing all their dreams of safety and prosperity.

Demagoguery and the Appeal to Popular Passions

Is Rick Warren of Saddleback Church a demagogue? On December 19, 2008, Kathryn Kolbert, head of People for the American Way, challenged President-elect Barack Obama's choice to have Warren offer the inaugural invocation. She claimed that Warren "is a divisive Religious Right demagogue" who "marginalizes and dehumanizes those who disagree with him—he does nothing to help unite Americans!" For this reason, she claims, he did not deserve such a public position of honor.[11] But holding to and preaching conservative positions on public issues does not make a person a demagogue. Jerry Falwell and Pat Robertson are not demagogues simply because they took to the airwaves to promote their conservative values.

Preachers become pulpit demagogues when they demonize one group of people as those who are responsible for the ills being experienced by parishioners or the larger parish to whom the preacher sees himself or herself responsible. They scapegoat a dissenting out-group while providing the in-group with a closed system of argument characterized by rigidity, suspicion, and polarization. We could name a long list of the usual suspects who have built entire ministries on what they are against and who they oppose. Other lists could be generated that name individuals responsible for tearing denominations and faith communities asunder in the name of serving an idealized vision of the truth. The real question, however, is not *who* but *why*. Why are we all so tempted to demonize the ideas of others in the name of purity and the validation of our own idea of the truth?

The theologian Reinhold Niebuhr provides an insightful response to that question. He argued that it is in human nature to make a god out of our own will to power, turning our version of what's true into an idol we serve. In *The Nature and Destiny of Man* he wrote:

> The fanatic fury of religious controversies, the hatred engendered in theological disputes, the bitterness of ecclesiastical rivalries and the pretentious claims of ecclesiastical dominion all reveal the continued power of sin in the life of the "redeemed"; and the use which sin makes of the pretension of holiness.[12]

One of these pretensions of holiness can be to turn our belief into dogmatism that becomes an all-consuming ideology. We humans all have implicit and sometimes explicit ideologies that shape our understanding of how to live in community with others.

Niebuhr was particularly interested in what happens when ideology becomes idolatry. Ideologies, like idolatries, are only partial accounts of much more complex realities. But an ideology, especially one that becomes an idolatry, can hide from its adherents their own lack of dependence on God and their sinful will to power. As a result these adherents can become ideologues of one true answer that restores the world to some idealized true way of life. For Niebuhr this will to power is the inevitable human effort to negate the fall in order to restore an idealized conception of peace and stability. It is always offered in the name of God but is achieved by asserting a will to power rather than a dependence on God.

Pastor Timothy Keller argues that this effort becomes idolatrous worship of a counterfeit god that offers an empty promise of deliverance. Keller reminds

particularly adept in treating argument like waging war, especially those who "take no prisoners," are often identified as Machiavellian. The difference between persuasion and use of coercion to manipulate listeners is lost on these people. They are willing to win whatever the cost, often by employing cunning and duplicity to achieve their purposes.

This is an exaggerated form of the kind of reasoning that Niccolò Machiavelli actually counseled his fictional prince to adopt in *The Prince*, published in 1532. He urged a new prince to act prudently in acquiring and keeping power, an approach to prudence that would involve making morally ambiguous choices when necessary. Power was treated as a scarce resource that must be guarded if the efforts of the Prince were to be successful. Though the work does not advocate the kind of ruthlessness described above, it does assume that the purpose of exercising influence is to win and accrue even greater power. And it is this same will to power that is at the heart of the temptation to engage in demagoguery.

The art of waging this kind of war of words and influence has cast a pall over the art of persuasion. For many, teaching people the art of persuasion is akin to teaching them how to use a sliding moral scale in which ruthlessness in achieving one's goal is always a live option. And there is a truth in that observation, since like any art, skill in communication can be used for either noble or ignoble ends. So how does a preacher know when the sickness to win at whatever the cost has taken over?

Persuasion has come upon hard times in preaching because it is so easy to abuse in this manner. In the fourth century church leaders forbade the use of rhetoric because it was an art designed to persuade people rather than prove truth. At the outset of the twenty-first century some Christian homileticians have argued that persuasion has no place in preaching, because it places human ends over God's purpose in the proclamation of the Word. We have already made a case why this is an unrealistic view of human communication in the first chapter, but we can understand why some people who love God and are passionate about their faith want nothing more to do with something they believe can too easily slide into pulpit demagoguery in the name of Christ.

We believe that understanding the role of persuasion needs to be redeemed in preaching by replacing the competitive metaphor with a collaborative one. Reliability with listeners is better achieved when we seek to woo rather than win them. The purpose of wooing is to seek a collaborative reception of faith in God rather than try to prove that claims of faith are superior to other worldviews. Persuasion is an art of influence rather than conquest.

For true persuasion to occur there must be an act of communication in which someone intends to influence others who have the ability to make judgments or make choices in response. So for a communicative act to be considered persuasion it cannot be coercive, impositional, or involve a quid-pro-quo exchange.[16] Manipulation occurs when one of these three ways of assuring acceptance of influence is added to the mix. For people to be persuaded they need to come by their belief honestly. The problem with demagogues is that they operate with a coercive win-at-any-cost form of rhetoric that turns persuasion into propaganda. In the next chapter we will discover that the Despot lacks faithfulness to the gospel by imposing a ruling from above. Yet demagogues, unlike despots, only have power as long as they have followers willing to listen.

Persuasion's real art is not captured best by the competitive vision of influence found in *The Prince*. Baldassare Castiglione's *Book of the Courtier*, published four years earlier in 1528, presented the ideas that dominated the Renaissance conception of effectiveness in the art of persuasion. If *The Prince* represents the definitive work on how to exercise power over others, *The Book of the Courtier* represents the definitive work on how to collaboratively court the assent of people.[17] Castiglione's protagonist, the Count, maintains that a prudent courtier is one who adopts *sprezzatura*, or a "certain nonchalance," in any effort to influence members of the court. "Accordingly we may affirm that to be true art," the Count suggests, "which does not appear to be art; nor to anything must we give greater care than to conceal art, for if it is discovered, it quite destroys our credit and brings us into small esteem."[18] He explains that, just as we are less inclined to admire the dancer who looks as if he is counting steps, we are also less influenced by one whose argument appears calculated. The goal of a courtier is to influence rather than triumph. To the strategies of "nonchalance" Castiglione also adds discretion, decorum, gracefulness, and *vergogna* (a shyness or honorableness that keeps one from shameful or embarrassing activity). These are counterstrategies to those of a demagogic rhetoric.

In proposing these virtuous strategies of wooing assent, we are not trying to reinstate the virtues of sixteenth-century court behavior as the model for twenty-first-century preaching. In fact, the various forms of the word *woo* that appear in *The Book of the Courtier* all refer to the art of courting the favor of a woman. What we choose to draw attention to is the manner in which Castiglione's art of influence is shaped more by a collaborative metaphor than by a competitive one. Contemporary usage of the word *woo* often moves beyond its original romantic association by focusing on this collaborative quality. A quick Internet search yielded the following news headlines:

- Democrats Try to Woo Consumer Advocate to Run
- Wal-Mart Tried to Woo City with Smaller Stores
- Obama Goes on Facebook to Woo Tech Industries
- Mavs Fans Try to Woo LeBron to Dallas with Website

Notice that such usage does not assume a scarce-resource orientation to the art of persuasion. Rather than treating assent as something to be won at someone else's loss, wooing is persuasion that seeks to join with the one whose assent is sought in arriving at a mutually useful response. We take up the use of woo because it represents a collaborative rather than a conquering approach to the art of influence. It takes two to woo.

As a virtue in preaching, Castiglione's counsel would be to woo

- through *sprezzatura*, exercising discretion, decorum, and gracefulness in one's style and substance while directing appeals toward others
- through *vergogna*'s sense of both honor and shame as that which shapes the moral boundaries of our civility toward others

Wooing's art of preaching gracefully is not the same as the work of grace that can occur as word of God in preaching. Yet wooing is much like the work of the Holy Spirit. Wooing invites and does not demand; wooing prizes mutuality rather than causality.

Woo in the Pulpit

What virtues would preaching that is not an escape from freedom seek to engender? Erich Fromm believed that cultures, like religions, serve to help people try to make meaning out of their lives. Virtuous cultures that help people negotiate the tensions of freedom address five basic human needs. They provide people with a sense of relatedness, transcendence, and rootedness. In addition they help people develop a sense of identity and provide them with a healthy frame of orientation.[19] Fromm derived these qualities from what productive religious faith provides. The Apostle Paul seeks to woo the people at Galatia not to live as people who do not return to the way of the Answer, but to live in the tensions created by the freedom they have been called to in Christ. Notice how the very themes Fromm develops are found in Paul's challenge to live into freedom as well:

> For you were called to freedom, brothers and sisters; only do not use your freedom as an opportunity for self-indulgence, but through love become slaves to one another. For the whole law is summed up in a single commandment, "You shall love your neighbor as yourself" [*relatedness*]. If, however, you bite and devour one another, take care that you are not consumed by one another. Live by the Spirit, I say, and do not gratify the desires of the flesh [*a sense of identity*]. For what the flesh desires is opposed to the Spirit, and what the Spirit desires is opposed to the flesh; for these are opposed to each other, to prevent you from doing what you want [*healthy frame orientation*]. But if you are led by the Spirit, you are not subject to the law [*rootedness*]. . . . If we live by the Spirit, let us also be guided by the Spirit [*transcendence*]. (Gal. 5:13-18, 25)

Drawing on the counsel of Paul and on Erich Fromm's summary of a healthy religious worldview, we believe preaching that woos people to live into the claims of Christ calls them to embrace the tensions of freedom and resist returning to the law, to the Answer, or to whatever other option represents an escape from freedom.

Niebuhr argued that when we are not sure we too often act as if we are doubly sure—the temptation that leads to the fanatic belief of fundamentalism. But it doesn't have to. Good doubt tempers blind faith. As Rabbi Brad Hirschfield observes about his own maturation in faith:

> I have been completely taken over by the intoxication of being "doubly sure." But I have come to know that the true meaning of faith is not to be found in these sureties or in a single absolute, but in *competing* absolutes. Faith is about a loving acceptance of the profound complexity of existence and creation. It is about abiding in mystery, in being unsure, while still being ready to act boldly.[20]

Striving to woo people to a reasoned reception of faith rejects the temptation to reduce the complexity and struggle of what it means to live faithfully in the world as people who trust God to be the Answer.

Preachers who strive to respect parishioners week in and week out help them cherish the tensions that make freedom of faith possible. They woo parishioners—collaborating with them by way of their pulpit practices—to realize what it means to live in relatedness with one another, in rootedness to a tradition of faith in God, and to discover transcendent meaning through dependence on God. They provide the means by which parishioners can be formed as the people of God (a sense of identity) who live in the realities of this world but live in relationship to others by the claims of another realm (healthy frame of orientation). In humility, they recognize that the desire for power can become an idol and that building a large following is not the same as serving the call to freedom or of being guided by the Spirit.

FOR FURTHER READING

Alan Brinkley. *Voices of Protest: Huey Long, Father Coughlin, and the Great Depression*. New York: Knopf, 1982.

Timothy Keller. *Counterfeit Gods: The Empty Promises of Money, Sex, and Power, and the Only Hope That Matters*. New York: Dutton, 2009.

Reinhold Niebuhr. *The Nature and Destiny of Man: Volume One, Human Nature*. New York: Scribner, 1964.

Chapter Seven

THE
🖎 DESPOT ⟩

In the spring of 2005, the Washington National Cathedral installed a new dean, who serves as the head of the cathedral. The new dean had invited an old friend, George Regas, to preach on Sunday, April 24, 2005, the day after the installation service. Regas was Rector Emeritus of All Saints Church in Pasadena known for preaching controversial sermons and taking liberal stands. His sermon in the Cathedral lived up to that reputation.

The title of Rev. Regas's sermon that morning was "Interpreting Christ in a Pluralistic World." In the opening of his sermon he told a story about a minister who thought he was being misunderstood. Regas observed, "There is nothing in the world more upsetting and disconcerting to a preacher than to have someone miss the mood and intent [of his sermon]."[1] Was there, we might wonder, a bit of foreshadowing in his comment? He went on to note that "this pulpit has been the place from which some of America's most searching and challenging proclamations have been made."[2] He said he wanted to continue that tradition by preaching against exclusivism and, in particular, Christian exclusivism. With John 14:1-14 as his text, Regas "personally reject[ed] the claim that Christianity has the truth and all other religious are in error."[3] But he did not stop there. He declared that "the Religious Right has drowned out everyone else with their absolutist claims. They have the truth and the rest of us are living under false claims." Because of them, he maintained, "faith in Jesus has come to be known as pro-rich, pro-war, and pro-American . . . Jesus has been hijacked and turned into the guardian of privilege instead of the champion of the dispossessed."[4]

Later in the sermon, when he pleaded, "I have more to say, so stay with me," it was already too late for the dozen or so who had walked out. Was Rev. Regas's goal to antagonize and anger the conservative Christians in attendance? Or, did they miss the "mood and intent" of his sermon? Rather than calling for those present to lay aside theological differences to join together in God's purposes, we think he was simply offering up Christian "road rage" in the pulpit. Castigating those with whom you disagree politically may be a way to get elected to a public office, but it is neither respectful of differences among listeners nor faithful to a calling to preach the gospel. We suspect that Regas believed he was standing in the line of the prophets and if his message angered his listeners, so be it. But this kind of preaching raises an important challenge. When do we cease to be prophetic in our preaching and simply become an arrogant pulpit despot? We are reminded of the comment made by an Oracle Corporation executive, offhandedly describing his narcissistic CEO, Larry Ellison: "The difference between God and Larry is that God does not believe he is Larry."[5]

Freud gave us the term *narcissist* from the mythical figure of Narcissus who was so pathologically enamored with his own image that he died because he couldn't turn his gaze away from it. The author of an award-winning *Harvard Business Review* essay on both the pros and cons of the narcissistic CEO writes that leaders such as Jack Welch and George Soros are examples of what he calls productive narcissists. They are risk-taking, hard-charging CEOs who get the job done while stirring the masses with their rhetoric. Narcissistic CEOs generally project personal charisma. They are rhetorically effective, capable of articulating grand visions. In the right position and at the right time, they can develop scores of followers. However, the danger is that they tend to "harbor the illusion that only circumstances or enemies block their success. This tendency toward grandiosity and distrust is the Achilles' heel of narcissism."[6]

Even the most brilliant narcissists are quite self-involved, unpredictable, and—in extreme cases—paranoid. The *HBR* essayist notes that narcissistic CEOs, whether successful or not, typically

- lack empathy—they are uncomfortable with their own emotions;
- are sensitive to criticism—they are uncomfortable with the emotive assessment of others;
- are poor listeners—they don't learn from others easily;
- dominate meetings—they have a distaste for collaborating or mentoring; and
- have an intense desire to compete—they do not tolerate dissenting opinions.

An argument can be made that at times of great turmoil, the narcissistic leader may be just what an organization needs to be more effective. But in the church? As Barbara Brown Taylor notes, "Baptism and narcissism cancel each other out."[7]

Most of us have met or know of clergy who are so arrogant in their pulpit practice that they have no problem determining why they are right and others are just dead wrong. They speak in superlatives and always know exactly what the truth is or what the answer should be. We call such people narcissists for a reason, and, in the right circumstances, we even call them despots. Narcissistic clergy, who become obsessed with wielding power, are particularly prone to become pulpit despots. Their will to power—their self-righteous belief that they alone know the truth—when wedded to a moral and spiritual theology of ultimate concern inevitably results in a toxic expression of religious intolerance. The size of the congregation is not the issue. Pulpit despots can be found in thirty-member congregations or in mega-churches.

Pulpit despots can also be found at both ends of the continuum of arrogance. But for reasons that will soon become obvious we will focus more on the extremes of toxic fundamentalism in this chapter. Yet toxic religion can manifest itself in a variety of ways that form temptations in the pulpit. One author has recently suggested that fundamentalism, anti-Semitism, triumphalism, and moralism in the pulpit should all be viewed equally as toxic expressions of Christianity.[8] We would add that emerging anti-Islamic attitudes in the pulpit are a kind of variation of the historic problem of anti-Semitism. We also think that "old liberal" bombastic arrogance like that of Rev. Regas, though perhaps not toxic spirituality, is still toxic arrogance. They are all markers of pulpit despots along with their inability to listen. In their hands the virtues of serving the persuasive resource of *logos* become narrowly focused on implementing one and only one way forward—the despot's way.

THE DESPOT AND THE PROBLEM OF SELF-RIGHTEOUSNESS

A despot is a tyrant, a person who wields absolute power, often in cruel and oppressive ways, or at least in ways that appear emotionally detached from how decisions may affect those governed.[9] Though the term *despot* originated in the Byzantine Empire, the Egyptian pharaoh is often held up as the classic example of a despot. Despotic governance may have one titular head like the pharaoh or a very tightly knit leadership oligarchy, but it is the singular focus of despots on advancing their power that defines this kind of rule.

Pulpit despots, like pulpit demagogues, operate with an assumption that truth is a scarce resource and that they are the one who should control its dissemination. But unlike pulpit demagogues who seek to exploit the beliefs and values of others in service to a narrow or toxic view of faith, pulpit despots self-righteously assume their truth justifies their leadership. They speak and act in an autocratic manner because they have utter faith they are right. On the one hand, the demagogue comes alive in his or her ability to move the masses—to have followers. And, in order to keep those followers, a demagogue will exploitatively adapt his or her message to whatever is needed to maintain, sustain, and continue to grow that following. Pulpit despots, on the other hand, never waver from their version of truth. It is inviolable; they self-righteously demand obedience to the message even to the point of declaring holy war to vindicate its truth.

The ethical problem with pulpit despots is that they rarely grasp how they have been co-opted by their own self-righteous dogmatism in their pastoral task. In the process of seeking to persuade others to support their single-minded understanding of "the faith," they often betray the very faith they seek to defend.

Leading the Sincere Astray

Charles Kimball has identified five warning signs of a corrupt religious worldview that get at the heart of the matter. Kimball argues that a form of the greatest commandment as summarized by Jesus can be found in all of the major religious traditions:

> "You shall love the Lord your God with all your heart, and with your soul, and with your mind." This is the greatest and first commandment. And a second is like it: "You shall love your neighbor as yourself." On these two commandments hang all the law and the prophets. (Matt. 22:37-40)

Jews, Hindus, Muslims, Buddhists, Christians, and those of other religions all affirm the intrinsic truth of the claim that love of God and love of neighbor is what marks us as people who live faithfully toward God and responsibly toward one another.[10] Violent or destructive actions taken against those who are different is a corruption of this most basic religious impulse. "When religion remains true to its authentic source," Kimball argues, "it is actively dismantling these corruptions, a process that is urgently needed now."[11]

What are these five warning signs? Pulpit despots responsible for turning a religious tradition into a toxic direction typically corrupt a practice or tension within a religious tradition in one or more of the following ways.

By Making Absolute Truth Claims

On March 10, 1993, Michael Griffin shot and killed Dr. David Gunn, a physician who provided abortions at a clinic in Pensacola, Florida. Five days later, Pastor Paul Hill appeared on Phil Donahue's television talk show to defend the actions of Michael Griffin. Over the course of the months that followed, Hill became so convinced by his own absolute truth claims defending Griffin's actions that fourteen months later at the same clinic in Pensacola, Florida, he shot and killed Dr. John Britton (and his traveling companion, James Barrett).[12] Hill is an ardent member of a national organization known as the Army of God. Griffin was deeply influenced by the truth claims of this movement—as was Scott Roeder, who shot and killed Dr. George Tiller in Wichita on May 31, 2009.[13]

There are many Christians who are strongly opposed to abortion on religious grounds. But only the extremists believe that it is acceptable to kill in order to stop the killing. The Army of God website, however, is filled with scriptural references attempting to validate this response. They identify Scott Roeder, Michael Griffin, and Paul Hill as American heroes and invite people to send thank-you notices to these men, praising them for their actions on behalf of faith, God, and the unborn children saved by their actions.

Abortion is a tragedy. Virtually all people of faith affirm this. Many believe it should never happen, while others concede that it is a terrible choice people sometimes find themselves forced to make. Using absolute truth to justify acts that compound the tragedy of abortion can only occur when a single moral value is allowed to trump all others. Add to this a recourse to absolute truth claims based on one's own analogical interpretation of biblical texts and the result, as in the case of Paul Hill, can lead people to justify a morally reprehensible means to express their grievance.[14] The grievance may be just. The pathway to resolve it is not.

By Demanding Blind Obedience

Asahara Shoko, founder of Aum Shinrikyo, was found guilty of directing followers of this faith to release deadly sarin nerve gas in a Tokyo subway on March 20, 1995. Thirteen people died during the incident, while Japan reported that thousands suffered various aftereffects. This was not a small movement. It had approximately 10,000 members in Japan and almost 30,000 followers in Russia.

During Asahara Shoko's trial, the prosecution argued that he was directly behind the attack because he wanted to create government instability, which would have allowed him the opportunity to ascend to the position of Emperor of Japan. The defense sought to argue that it was several of Asahara Shoko's followers who were responsible for the attack rather that Shoko. Though there were irregularities in the trial, it became clear that this was a religion that required unquestioning obedience from followers. The leader presented himself as one who had already experienced enlightenment, as a quasi-divine figure whose teachings should be accepted without question. It was difficult given this religious worldview to make an argument that Asahara Shoko had not been responsible for the sarin attack.

We could turn to a similar story examining how Reverend Jim Jones was able to demand the same obedience from followers in the Guyana compound where 638 adults and 276 children died as mass murder-suicide victims. Jones argued that he had ascended to a divine status that transcended that of the "sky-God." He provided his followers with tangible proof that he could answer prayers in ways that the sky-God never had, which is why he had the right to demand blind obedience. The point here is that despotic religious discourse typically requires unquestioning obedience from followers.

By Establishing the Ideal Time

Although some religious worldviews tend to look to the past when the religious ideals of their heritage were first received, there is an impulse in most religious worldviews to look to a time in the future when this ideal will be realized more fully. It may take on the form of a dispensational theology in Christianity in which some individual becomes famous for having interpreted the signs that prove we are about to arrive at the apocalyptic moment. In the 1970s, it was Hal Lindsey, then in the 1990s, Tim LaHaye. And most recently it was Christian radio broadcaster Harold Camping. He originally predicted that judgment day would be May 21, 1988, then September 6, 1994, then May 21, 2011, and finally October 21, 2011.

Though we may point to people who unwisely based financial decisions on Camping's beliefs, such prognostications are not a red flag by themselves. They take on more serious dimensions in the hands of someone such as Pat Robertson and other Christian Coalition leaders, who seek to change laws and propose legislative initiatives that support a Dominion Theology worldview. Their eschatology strongly supports the nation of Israel, to the point of disenfranchising Palestinians, the Middle Eastern group of people among whom Christianity has found its most welcome reception. And though this theology supports the Israeli state, it does so with a view of ushering in the promised end of time—a concern that Robertson has devoted himself to since the outset of his television program.

This zeal to establish the ideal time was tragically realized by Marshall Applewhite and the Heaven's Gate religious community. In March 1997, thirty-nine members "exited their bodies" in a mass suicide in order to escape the bonds of earth and have their souls taken aboard a spacecraft hidden in the contrail of the comet Hale-Bopp that was passing by earth at that time. He argued that the civilizations currently on earth are about to be "recycled" and that he was the embodiment of the second coming of Jesus Christ here to deliver followers from being "plowed under" at the end of this age.[15] Applewhite's identification of the ideal time went far beyond the eschatological forecasting engaged in by Robertson or by Camping, but his concern with identifying the advent of the age to come demonstrates what can happen when attention to this dimension of a theological tradition becomes all consuming.

By Preaching That the Ends Justify Any Means

The Westboro Baptist Church, headed by Pastor Fred Phelps, is widely regarded as a hate organization because its Kansas-based members aggressively picket the funerals of U.S. soldiers. They maintain that the deaths of these soldiers stand as a witness of God's judgment on this nation for its tolerance of homosexuality. They have picketed funerals of prominent citizens of other religious groups (Catholics, Jews, other Christian denominations, and so on) and sporting, entertainment, and civic events in order to speak prophetically to their community and to the world.

The seventy or so members of this congregation adopt an extreme Calvinist, antimissionary perspective. They are not on street corners to win followers; they are there to witness to what they believe is the truth of God's judgment on this nation and the world. They have taken the hyper-Calvinist teaching of the Primitive Baptist sect to the next step, justifying their actions as prophetic witness against hell-bound people. Hell-bound people are those who do not follow the teachings and beliefs of their congregation. In their system of belief in limited atonement, Christ died only for the elect few who are committed to the beliefs of Westboro Baptist Church and what it stands against.

They are simultaneously contemptuous of the media as part of the scourge of American depravity and dependent on it to publicize their witness. They are contemptuous of the American judicial system but also confident that it will protect their right to free speech. The inherent contradiction of their contempt for the very institutions they depend upon is deemed irrelevant because the ends of their prophetic witness documented by the media and protected by the laws justify the extremes of their insensitive practices.

By Declaring Holy War

Jessica Stern, the foremost U.S. expert on terrorists, writes, "Holy wars take off only when there is a large supply of young men who feel humiliated and deprived; when leaders emerge who know how to capitalize on those feelings; and when a segment of society—for whatever reason—is willing to fund them."[16] Osama bin Laden and Al-Qaida leadership were able to reach followers in this way. That's why it may surprise readers that we class Pastor Terry Jones as engaging in the same practice he condemns among the jihadists. Why? People who have no knowledge of Jones's beliefs or activities have died because he declared holy war against people who are Muslim. Far from being a well-financed terrorist (Jones has only about thirty to forty members in his Dove World Outreach Center in Gainseville, Florida), he depends on media coverage to accomplish his purpose. In July 2010, Pastor Jones declared holy war against Islam by announcing his intention to burn two hundred copies of the Quran at his outreach center on September 11, 2010.

Religious and secular leaders pleaded with Pastor Jones not to follow through with this promise. President Obama made a public statement to this end: "If he's listening, I just hope he understands that what he's proposing to do is completely contrary to our values. . . . I just want him to understand that this stunt that he is pulling could greatly endanger our young men and women in uniform who are in Iraq, who are in Afghanistan."[17] Twenty people were already dead because Jones had announced his intention to burn the Quran.

Jones initially acceded to these appeals, but a few months later he decided to "stand for the truth" and publicly burned the Quran. When his actions became known, the *New York Times* reported that 9 people were killed and 90 others were injured in a Kandahar protest while 30 people were killed—including 7 U.N. employees—and 150 people were injured in a protest attack on the U.N. Assistance Mission compound in Mazar-i-Sharif, Afghanistan. Nations and religious groups have expressed outrage at the burning of the Quran. Al-Fallujah, a Web forum that defends Islamic jihad, posted a threat calling for "rivers" of American blood to flow in response to this sacrilege.[18] Members of Westboro Baptist Church lodged a protest of their own. They had already burned the Quran two years earlier. Their spokeswoman stated that it was unfair that Jones was getting public attention for something they had already done.[19]

The Wikipedia article on this event provides a list of far-right religious sects and individuals who plan to engage in similar acts directed against Islam. These individuals may have been appalled by Westboro's hyper-Calvinist witness at the funerals of fallen U.S. soldiers, but Pastor Jones's protest has sparked their imagination. They see in it a way to publicly express their feelings of rage and impotence as the culture changes around them. Jessica Stern is correct. Pulpit despots can direct hatred that fuels a holy war even if they are just a pastor of a thirty-member church.

The Pulpit Despot

We have provided a list of the most egregious of sinners in this chapter. These are people who, in the name of God, have truly become "rotten with perfection."[20] And it is in this sense that pulpit despotism is a hardening of dogmatism's arteries—logos as end rather than as means of persuasion. This kind of hardening of the arteries occurs whenever intolerant leaders demand allegiance to ends that lead astray people who are sincere in their faith.

Despots can be found in organizations of all sizes. It's likely that you have met a few despots of the pulpit along the way as well. They can be found wherever preachers offer as the word of God, a univocal interpretive meaning, privileging one and only one interpretation of the biblical text (usually their own) as the final, only, right interpretation of the word of God. The despot speaks for God and provides answers true for all times and all places. Pulpit despots are always sincere. They believe what they preach. If caught in a contradiction, they will often affirm the truth of what they have claimed all the more deeply, while a demagogue, like a manipulator, caught in the same dilemma is more likely to distance himself or herself from the original statement. But, as Kimball wisely notes, sincerity does not exempt people or groups from critical scrutiny or from accountability for their toxic reading of their religious tradition.[21]

Pulpit despots prey upon popular prejudices and make false claims and promises in order to gain power. They lose sight of what it means to name God and name grace in the life of a community of faith. They become narcissistically intoxicated with their own self-righteous agenda to stand for the truth, to rid the world of some great sin, or to witness to the world concerning God's judgment of it. They typically believe they have been chosen by God to scapegoat the group they have elected to vilify and to stand for God's truth. They present truth as nailed down into a set of answers—answers that they provide. What gets lost in this is Jesus' claim that true religion consists of loving "the Lord your God with all your heart, and with your soul, and with your mind . . . [and loving] your neighbor as yourself."

 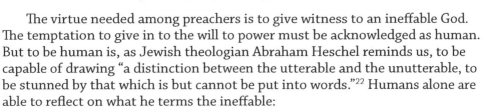

THE VIRTUE OF BEING A "NAMER OF GOD"

The virtue needed among preachers is to give witness to an ineffable God. The temptation to give in to the will to power must be acknowledged as human. But to be human is, as Jewish theologian Abraham Heschel reminds us, to be capable of drawing "a distinction between the utterable and the unutterable, to be stunned by that which is but cannot be put into words."[22] Humans alone are able to reflect on what he terms the ineffable:

> What smites us with unquenchable amazement is not that which we grasp and are able to convey but that which lies within our reach but beyond our grasp; not the quantitative aspect of nature but something qualitative; not what is beyond our range in time and space but the true meaning, source, and end of being, in other words, the ineffable.[23]

The call to serve God through a pulpit ministry must be approached with this kind of humility and awe rather than with arrogance and impatience. Preachers who embrace the virtue of being a "namer of God" surrender the need to nail truth down because they live with this sense of radical amazement about their calling to name the ineffable mystery of God and God's grace made evident in the world. For a "namer of God," words finally fail and yet must be found to translate the ministry of reconciliation with which we have been entrusted (2 Cor. 5:19).[24]

Heschel writes that "the awareness of the ineffable is that with which our search must begin . . . , [for] without the sense of the ineffable there are no metaphysical problems, no awareness of being as being, of value as value."[25] Such a claim on our soul demands that radical amazement is the appropriate response. We must balance reason with wonder because "God cannot be distilled to a well-defined idea." Rather, we are invited to communicate a sense of the divine, which is a message that discloses unity where we see diversity, that discloses peace when we are involved in discord. God is He who holds our fitful lives together, who reveals to us what is empirically diverse in color, in interests, in creeds—races, classes, nations—as one in His eyes and one in essence.[26]

This is God with us—the notion that we are never alone, never apart from God.

A preacher whose preaching is characterized by a deep sense of radical amazement and a deep awareness of the ineffability of God will not fall victim to the sin of arrogance and impatience that gives rise to a pulpit despot. In humility, a preacher will envision his or her task to be one of naming God and naming grace. Naming God involves bringing theological reflection to an interpretation of our world and the preacher's convictions about the meaning of biblical texts as they relate to God's purpose and this ineffable mystery of the divine. Naming grace involves bringing that same theological reflection to identifying and bringing before the eyes of others the experience of the holy in the lives of people with whom we share community and to whom we are called to witness.[27]

Naming Grace and Naming God

In the Christian tradition, this humility before the mystery that acknowledges radical astonishment and awareness of the ineffability of God would likely be given voice as a sacramental awareness of the holiness of life. In *Naming Grace: Preaching and the Sacramental Imagination*, Mary Catherine Hilkert writes, "The mystery of preaching is at once the proclamation of God's Word and the naming of grace in human experience."[28] She qualifies what preachers must sacramentally become aware of in naming grace in the lives of people:

- Experiences of grace named must be human experience in their depths.
- Experiences of grace must be named in the face of and yet in spite of human suffering.
- Experiences of grace named must echo the gospel story and the symbols of Christian tradition.

And preachers who offer this witness must name expressions of the grace of God about us to make its reality present to us and then name the power that makes that grace possible. Naming grace has as its purpose to be a witness who becomes a "namer of God."

Preachers who become a "namer of God" will avoid making absolute truth claims. It is often difficult for Christians to grasp the difference between the authority of Scripture as a written text and its interpretation. Anyone looking at a commentary on a biblical text or at sermons on these texts from 150 or 200 years ago and then at commentaries and sermons on these same texts today will quickly see just how different the emphases are that capture the attention of those reflecting theologically on this material. This is not to suggest that texts can mean anything. Far from it. It is tradition, text, and community that come together in our preaching. Our sermonic reflection always includes both the touchstone of the text itself, a tradition of interpretation, and the salience of that text's expression of truth as a way of approaching faith in God. The task of theology is to help people of faith realize that this is good. Much like translators who look to discover a dynamic equivalent when rendering the words of the Scriptures, preachers who seek the virtue of naming God will make sure that they never treat Holy Scripture as if it offers truth cut off from its ties to a living community. When that sad event happens, the result is often that the biblical text "gets reduced to a cadaver handed over for autopsy."[29] Answers are offered as if they are scientific facts rather than ineffable truths.

Preachers who become a "namer of God" will embrace Jesus' model of engaging listeners with stories, parables, questions, and teaching that calls for living into an extravagant moral ideal of God's purposes. Radical amazement does not evoke blind obedience. What it does evoke is awareness of the holiness of God, the sameness of the other, and the sacredness of life. Of course obedience is not the problematic term here. As the old revival hymn reminds us, "Trust and obey / For there's no other way / To be happy in Jesus / But to trust and obey."

This call to obedience is like the call to seek first the ways of God and his righteousness (Matt. 6:33); it's a call to be willing to be a servant to the needs of others rather than to simply seek first our own needs. The problem is with the adjective *blind*. Jesus' call to discipleship assumes dialogue and coming-to-understanding as the way of faith. There is no virtue in blind obedience; it is not a synonym for faith. Faith may transcend the convictional understanding of mere belief, but it should never involve the choice of unquestioning obedience. That is the demand of those whose idol is the will to power.

Preachers who become a "namer of God" will eschew a preoccupation with identifying the ideal time, or the Day or time of the Lord. Otherworldly hope is a part of the narrative of every major religious tradition; implicit in the theologies of a religious worldview is the belief in the brokenness of creation as we currently experience it and the commitment to strive toward developing spiritual disciplines that characterize the life of the ideal realm of God. But a cornerstone of belief among some conservative religious groups, especially American Dispensationalism and American Reconstructionist theology (including its variation of Dominion theologies), is the concern to join together with God in ushering in the Day of the Lord. This joining together involves taking political action consonant with establishing a promised eschatological theocracy on earth. All people of faith, especially those in the Judeo-Christian-Muslim tradition, place faith in God's sovereign purpose in history. They all pray some variation of the invitation, "Thy Kingdom come, Thy will be done on earth as it is in heaven." They are careful, however, to avoid engaging in cabalistic efforts to finally name God's time. Jessica Stern concludes:

> The religious terrorists we face are fighting us on every level—militarily, psychologically, and spiritually. Their military weapons are powerful, but spiritual dread is the most dangerous weapon in their arsenal. Perhaps the most truly evil aspect of religious terrorism is that it aims at destroying moral distinctions themselves.[30]

Preachers who become a "namer of God" refuse to engage in the rhetoric of intolerance in the pulpit, refuse to support arguments with ends proving the rightness of our own group that then justify intolerant means directed toward people who are different than we are. They take a stand rooted in the commitments of their theological tradition while finding language to reach out to those who are different. They acknowledge a theology of common grace that can find the wonder of God in difference and in people whose beliefs and customs are different than our own. A "namer of God" listens for opportunities to present stories that express unity in diversity. They do not permit language that erases moral distinctions in the name of privileging one heritage, one worldview, or one tribe.

Preachers who become a "namer of God" will acknowledge with Miroslav Volf that the cry to remember the wrongs done to us is natural and human, but the call for reconciliation is divine. The call to be reconciled to those who have sinned against us or with those against whom we have sinned is at the center of Christian faith and the practice of eucharistic communion with God. For unless we are willing to forgive others, we are told, there can be no forgiveness for us (Matt. 6:14-15). People of faith must rigorously guard against permitting revenge narratives a place "under the mantle of a religiously sanctioned struggle for the faith, for self-protection, for national preservation, for our way of life—all in the name of God and accompanied by celebration of the self sacrificial love of Christ!"[31] There is no place in a community of faith that names God and names grace to declare holy war.

There are ways that we can remember wrongs wrongly, and there are ways to remember them rightly. For reconciliation to be real in our practice of faith, Volf argues, it must be acknowledged that it occurs at its best when we participate in a faith community that does not nurse resentments in order to extract revenge. In faithful Christian communities in which reconciliation is sought as part of participating in a practice of communion or the observance of the Eucharist, the final judgment should set the pattern for seeking forgiveness. In the final judgment of God reconciliation will become manifest:

- People's sins, in all their magnitude, against God and neighbor must be brought to light by the judgment of grace.

- God will right all wrongs, settle all cases, since all sins against another or sins against us are ultimately sins against God.

- As judged peoples we will then see one another in the eyes of Christ and whatever remnants of resentment and revenge we may have yet harbored will be surrendered in a final mutual embrace that acknowledges the justice of God.[32]

Neither sin nor the remembrance of wrongs nurtured as injustices unresolved has any place in the embrace of reconciliation we long to receive in that day.

We began this chapter by examining liberal arrogance that has lost sight of being faithful to gospel claims. We then examined the extremes of toxic fundamentalism as exemplars of the sin of pulpit despotism. And here we end with an invitation to comprehend the necessary virtue of humility in the face of the final judgment's vision of what it means to preach reconciliation (2 Cor. 5:19). Though some may wish to quibble over who will actually participate in the redemption of judgment's "final embrace," we are still called by Christ to leave such questions with God and live as people who forgive. If we are to live into the faithfulness of our gospel calling, the challenge to become "namers of God" will require that radical amazement should be our response to the grace offered to us by an ineffable God.

FOR FURTHER READING

Abraham Heschel. *Man Is Not Alone: A Philosophy of Religion*. New York: Farrar, Straus and Giroux, 1976.

Mary Catherine Hilkert. *Naming Grace: Preaching and the Sacramental Imagination*. New York: Continuum, 2000.

Charles Kimball. *When Religion Becomes Evil: Five Warning Signs*. New York: HarperOne, 2008.

Miroslav Volf. *The End of Memory: Remembering Rightly in a Violent World*. Grand Rapids: Eerdmans, 2006.

Chapter Eight

WAIT! WAIT!
ᚖTHERE'S MORE!ᚔ

Recently, Bob heard a pastor preach on the biblical concept of peace from Philippians 4:4-7. The order of worship was printed on a folded 8½-x-11-inch piece of paper, but the cover design was original art, possibly found on the Internet. It had an artistic depiction of the lion and the lamb on the cover, and the visual was surrounded by words attributed to Helen Keller: "I do not want the peace which passeth understanding, I want the understanding which bringeth peace." During the service a lay reader read the biblical text:

> Rejoice in the Lord always; again I will say, Rejoice. Let your gentleness be known to everyone. The Lord is near. Do not worry about anything, but in everything by prayer and supplication with thanksgiving let your requests be made known to God. And the peace of God, which surpasses all understanding, will guard your hearts and your minds in Christ Jesus.

Clearly Helen Keller's clever aphorism took issue with Paul's claim, at least in terms of the kind of peace she really longed for. The listening parishioners were ready to hear how the provocative pairing of these two ideas might give insight to living faithfully that week. It clearly raised the question, "What should count as a Christian understanding of peace?"

The problem? The Keller quotation was never mentioned in the sermon. The parishioners who noticed the quotation were left to wonder why this provocative counsel was highlighted only to be ignored. Likely, it was an unthinking mistake, a picture with a quotation grabbed from the Internet by the office administrator who put the worship folder together based on a sermon text provided by the pastor. It is unclear whether the pastor even knew the quotation was on the cover let alone be held accountable to engage it. Unfortunately, the question posed by the pairing was more interesting than the sermon Bob heard. The sermon was primarily a collection of several inspiring stories of people who personally experienced God's peace offered to assure listeners that God's peace is possible for them as well.

Far from being irresponsible or even a misstep, however, we would class the disconnect in this story as a simple unthinking mistake, what we might call a preaching misdemeanor. Unthinking mistakes—like the mixed message between the worship folder and sermon—tend to be isolated occurrences rather than conscious choices. Unthinking mistakes happen all the time. It was practically a crisis in ministry for Bob when his very young, newly hired office worker decided to abbreviate the third word of the Women's Missionary Association to just three letters in the announcements on the back of the order of worship. Unthinking mistakes are neither mortal nor venial sins. They are just mistakes.

Recall that what we call missteps are those pulpit behaviors in which the preacher is aware she or he has chosen to accept or settle for engaging in a practice that too often becomes a bad habit in preaching. Developing these negative habits is the first step to accepting pulpit behavior that can lead to irresponsible preaching.

AN ABECEDARIUM OF MISSTEPS

We can't imagine a preacher who hasn't had that moment in the middle of a sermon when her stomach dropped, cringing inside with the thought, "Oh no, what did I just say?" It could have been an offhand comment inserted at that moment. Or it could have been the realization that the sermon she had written just wasn't fitting the listeners seated in front of her.

Did that preacher commit a mortal sin? Was a trip to the confessional in order? Probably not. But our preaching has been, is, and will forever be filled with these venial missteps and momentary lapses to which we are wise to be attentive.

In previous chapters we introduced you to a number of irresponsible offenders who unfortunately populate today's pulpits. The following portraits aren't as egregious, but they constitute a list of poor practices. Let's just call what follows the A, B, Cs of missteps.

A Is for Agitate or Aggravate

For every congregation and every listener there will always be controversial issues. Some will be national or international political debates, others local disagreements. It is the rare congregation that is not embroiled in some conflict, large or trivial.

When Lucy was first ordained she was the assistant at a church that discussed, at every vestry meeting (the leadership council in the Episcopal Church), what to do with a ditch that ran alongside the church property. Some years later she was speaking with the current rector and asked him if they were still arguing about the ditch. He assured her that, after many years, they had finally come to a resolution. However, the disagreements had gone on for so long the entries in the vestry minutes finally came to refer to it not as the ditch but the "damned ditch."

Although we do not want to suggest that preachers should not discuss those issues from the pulpit (although it was never a temptation to discuss the "damned ditch"), we would suggest that it is a misstep to raise political or controversial issues in passing: to, in effect, wave a red flag before a congregation's eyes and then move blithely on.

If we are going to raise or mention one of these controversial, contentious red-flag issues, it needs to be for a specific reason that actually advances the focus of the sermon, or we shouldn't do it. When red-flag issues are raised in our sermons we need to give people an opportunity at some point to respond to the issue we have raised, perhaps in a discussion group following the service. When we agitate or aggravate, when we wave red flags, people's attention and energies are quickly directed away from our message. They lose track of the purpose of our sermon and focus on why the flag justifies, irritates, or angers them.

Our advice? Wave those red flags carefully, judiciously, and intentionally.

B Is for Bore

We bore our listeners when we make great and amazing gospel stories seem dull and uninteresting. The Scriptures are filled with fascinating people who did amazing things. But if we make them come across as two-dimensional cardboard cutouts, then our listeners will find it difficult to become enthusiastic about or engaged with these crucial stories.

A friend told of a sermon she heard on the opening of Mark's Gospel and John the Baptist's declaration that he was not worthy "to stoop down and untie the thong of [Jesus'] sandals" (Mark 1:7). Although the preacher and congregation were presented with an amazing picture of the voice crying in the wilderness—proclaiming that a powerful servant of God was coming to "baptize you with the Holy Spirit" (Mark 1:8)—the preacher lost sight of the big picture. She said that for fifteen minutes he gave them a lesson on sandals. She learned a great deal about sandals in the biblical world, but she could never figure out what that had to do with John or Jesus or her. Needless to say, she grew quite bored. Preachers who bore listeners are either already bored themselves or really need to get out more.

We bore our listeners if we get so entangled in our exegesis and scholarly interests that we forget that there must be a larger "so what" to our sermon. People do not come to church wondering what exegesis reveals. As Harry Emerson Fosdick reportedly asked, "Could any procedure be more surely predestined to dullness and futility. . . . Only the preacher proceeds still upon the idea that folk come to church desperately anxious to discover what happened to the

Jebusites."[1] The story of the Jebusites can be interesting, maybe even intriguing, but it must be put in the larger service of the concern to which the sermon is focused.

Lucy recently heard a sermon during which the preacher declared repeatedly that he knew we were probably tired of hearing him tell us over and over again, "God loves us." How, Lucy wondered, could we ever tire of hearing that great good news? Could it be that the preacher was projecting? If we think people are becoming bored with the message at the heart of the gospel, the problem is more likely that we lack the imagination to express it in different ways. Is it possible the preacher who projects boredom on the part of the people listening may be projecting boredom with his own call?

C Is for Confuse

As Lucy was once reminded by a student, "We don't want to preach three stories searching for a point." It's already too easy for listeners to lose their way in a sermon. Too many preachers forget that listening is a challenging and difficult skill. We work very hard these days to teach children the skills of reading and writing, but we assume that listening (or for some, watching) comes naturally. It does not.

If we are reading a book and don't understand a passage, we can go back and read the passage over and over and, if needed, over again. We don't have the luxury of asking a speaker/preacher to stop and explain what she or he meant. Bob remembers that in a pastorate he served, services were moved to an earlier hour for summer, and a sermon talk-back time was added following the sermon. Parishioners asked lots of questions. Attendance grew. Bob even considered making this order of events (worship first then education) a permanent design, but the congregation leaders were unwilling to make such a drastic change. Too bad. Looking back, he believes that it could have really led to growth for that congregation. At the same time he also learned that what he thought was wonderfully clear in a sermon could be quite confusing or at least raise lots of questions for people who bring different understandings of God and faith to a worship context.

As preachers we must keep our listeners in mind. We are going to take them on a journey. We know where we are going; they do not. We must make sure that we are focused and that our transitions are clear. Our listeners will appreciate it if we use previews to give them an idea of where we are going.

As listeners we are easily distracted. We might be distracted by a noise that we hear, or our minds might begin to wander. We might also be engaged and challenged by something that the preacher says and spin off thinking about that, only to find that the preacher has moved on and we have no idea what she is talking about. Therefore, previews and reviews help listeners contextualize and give them time to catch up.

D Is for Dull Delivery

It's the rare preacher who has had a voice class or a performance practices seminar. Therefore, too many preachers today think that amplification covers a multitude of sins. The fact that you are speaking into a microphone does not turn you into a good speaker.

Speaking to a large group of people is very different from speaking one on one, and poor delivery equates with poor preaching. A preacher can write a beautiful, well-crafted, engaging sermon, but if he mumbles or if she speaks in a boring monotone, the sermon will be dead on arrival. Following the style of the previous chapters, we were tempted to call these missteps "the Mumbler" or "Mr. Monotonous," but the real issue is simply dull delivery.

Many preachers believe that it is crucial today to have an informal, conversational preaching style. Delivery is definitely culturally determined, but even if you want to affect a casual style, you must still keep your listeners in mind.

First, the preacher must be aware of simple physics. The speed of sound is slower than the speed of light. We have experienced this reality when we see the flash of lightning long before hearing the rumble of thunder. That means that when we speak to a group larger than an individual standing in front of us, we must give the sound waves that we generate time to reach the people in the back row.

Lucy has had to learn this in a challenging space. She is a priest in the Episcopal Diocese of Washington, DC, and has preached at the Cathedral Church of St. Peter and St. Paul, also known as the National Cathedral. It is quite an experience to step into the pulpit of the cathedral. In addition to being a humbling experience when one thinks of the holy people who have preached from that pulpit, one realizes how far, far, far away people in the back rows are. Yes, there is a sound system, and quite a good one; however, the people in those back rows are at least two blocks away. It means that preachers who speak from that pulpit must slow down their rate of speech, giving that sound wave time to reach the back of the cathedral.

Second, good delivery requires that all preachers monitor their rate of speech. Remember you can speak faster than we can listen. You must also attend to your phrasing and inflection. Delivered speech is almost like singing. Through our phrasing and inflection we not only keep people's attention but also help them understand what is important.

Speakers must also be aware of their articulation. We must be sure to pronounce all of the sounds. In our everyday speech we have the tendency to get sloppy and drop sounds at the end of words and phrases. But if we do that in our preaching our listeners will have to guess at what we are saying.

God has called you to bring tidings of great news to all people. Make sure that all of those people can both hear and understand that good news.

E Is for Egregious Examples

On a cold, snowy Sunday in February, a congregation sat listening to a preacher. At the midpoint of the sermon she turned to an example of mowing the lawn. Mowing the lawn? Really? In February?

Virtually everyone sitting there lost the point of the illustration and the sermon as they realized their lawns were covered in snow. Why not talk about shoveling the sidewalk? It would have been a perfectly acceptable alternative example. Nothing tips the congregation off to the fact that they are getting a recycled sermon faster than an out-of-date or out-of-context illustration.

Examples and illustrations prove to be occasions for many a misstep. Again, we can count many different reasons:

- Out of Context. As in the case of the snowy Sunday reference to lawn-mowing, an example or illustration does not fit the time of year or location. Then again, even in February, the example of lawn-mowing probably works better than shoveling the walk in Florida.

- Out of Touch. Is the example something that listeners are familiar with? Jesus recognized that when he was speaking with those who fished he used one set of images. When he was speaking with those who kept sheep and goats he switched his metaphors. Nets worked with one group; gates and wolves with another. For many, references to Facebook and Twitter will be a wonderful way to connect with Jesus' call to go into "all the world." Yet those references will mean little to congregations that have resisted the technological transformation of daily life.

- TMI. Does the example give us "too much information"? Lucy attended a wedding at which the preacher stepped over the TMI line. What made it even more egregious was that the wedding was taking place at the principal Sunday morning worship service of the congregation. This was not a Friday- or Saturday-evening wedding with only adult guests. There were children and young people present in this service. The preacher wanted to share how wonderful marriage was, and, since the couple before him was older, he wanted to share with everyone how sexual relations got even better the older we get. Did we really need to know that? Projecting? TMI.

- Wholly Inappropriate. Some stories may be too grizzly or gruesome for the sermon. Bob's spouse, Barbara, grew up in fundamentalism. To this day she vividly remembers the "Hell Is Worse Than . . ." sermon she heard. The most vivid illustration was that hell is worse than being buried up to your head in tarmac and watching the asphalt paver rolling at you. And that was just one of many gruesome illustrations the pastor came up with to try to scare the hell out of listeners—literally. We may groan, but everyone can tell their own stories of unbelievably gruesome or grizzly stories that preachers still tell even though they should know better.

- Insensitivity. It is not the job of the pastor to out-parent the parents. Although you may know that there is no Santa Claus, be careful around Christmas. Young ears are listening. Don't let that information slip. Do not step over this line! We know of a priest who viewed it as his duty to set the children straight and remind them what Christmas was really about. From the pulpit he told all of the parish children—kindergarteners to eighth graders—that there was no Santa Claus. His voice mail was full before he had even taken off his vestments. We believe he should have headed straight for the confessional.

- Lack of Variety. Sports illustrations can be wonderful, but not if those are the only illustrations you use. Believe it or not, there are people in the pews who literally have no idea which sport is played by some of the teams you name. Though he may get e-mail for inappropriate stereotyping, Bob suggests that fellow male clergy consider the appeal if every other sermon from a female pastor had an illustration that began, "Why just the other day I was out shopping and . . ." Our point is to remember you have old, young, women, and men seated before you. Try to find things that will reach all of them.

Whole books have been written on use of sermon illustrations. We have but touched the surface here.

F Is for Fountain of Wisdom

If some preachers think people can't wait to learn about what happened to the Jebusites or what kinds of sandals John the Baptist may have been referring to, there are also preachers who fall into the trap of believing that it's their job to be the resident expert on whatever the topic du jour in the world is. These preachers want sermons to address contemporary rather than archaeological interest. They want more than anything to be relevant (see chapter 5 on the sin of pandering). They want to be the first to land on some topic or sermon series topic addressing whatever they think the pressing issue of the day is for parishioners. In other words, they believe their calling is to be a fountain of wisdom, personally providing answers for people on which to base their lives.

Fosdick argued that this was just as problematic as being the deadly dull preacher. He remarked:

> Week after week one sees these topical preachers who turn their pulpits into platforms and their sermons into lectures, straining after some new, intriguing subject; and one knows that in private they

are straining after some new, intriguing ideas about it. One knows also that no living man can weekly produce first-hand, independent, and valuable judgments on such an array of diverse themes, covering the whole range of human life. And, deeper yet, one who listens to such preaching or reads it knows that the preacher is starting at the wrong end.[2]

Fosdick's advice was that preachers need to remain true to their calling to preach from the Bible. The task, he believed, is to connect how that biblical story spoke a word of truth and meaning for the people when it was first uttered and to then grasp how that text speaks that word for people today. That is preaching that connects with people's needs, but needs identified by God's word rather than the world's worries.

MORE MISSTEPS OR LAPSES IN JUDGMENT

Before we cross the abecedarium line of finding a misstep, regardless of how obscure, for every letter of the alphabet, we think it wise to group a few more obvious problems with preaching. There's always more.

Sheep or Giraffes?

The story is often told of the woman who grasped the preacher's hand as she was exiting the church after worship and looked into his eyes. "Remember preacher," she implored, "Jesus told you to feed the sheep, not the giraffes." This kind soul wanted her pastor to remember that the vocabulary he chose needed to fit the congregation with whom he was speaking.

The vocabulary mismatch is often an issue for newly minted preachers fresh out of seminary. After several years of immersing themselves in academia and its specialized jargon, they forget that not everyone is familiar with *pericope*, *eschaton*, or *apocryphal*. There is nothing wrong with these words. As Kathleen Norris points out in her book *Amazing Grace*, they are wonderful words; we should use them and educate our listeners to the depth of their theologically rich meaning. However, not only are they meaningless out of context, but also we are being irresponsible if we toss them out at our listeners in order to impress. If we do use them, we need to ask whether they are actually necessary or whether we are still unknowingly trying to get approval from a now distant seminary professor. Likewise, as noted earlier with the preacher who became enamored with antique sandals, preachers can become too intrigued with specialized, arcane details of great interest to scholars but not so interesting to the average congregation.

The Snarky Commentator

Comedian Don Rickles is a master of insult. His jokes always come at the expense of others. Unfortunately, too many people practice this in their preaching as well. In an attempt to create camaraderie with listeners, as well as a sense of superiority over and against those being insulted or demeaned, the preacher makes fun of a person or group of people.

Lucy finds that it is crucial to stop this habit at the very start of her preaching classes. During the first class session she invites students to introduce themselves and to include information about their religious history and current affiliation. It is not uncommon for a student to identify himself as a "recovering fundamentalist" or herself as a "recovering Catholic." Lucy quickly reminds that person, and the rest of the class, that there may be a very faithful fundamentalist or Catholic in the class and that comment has just insulted and excluded that person.

Although we may not agree with another person or group, politically, theologically, or aesthetically, there is no excuse to dismiss or disparage others in our sermon. When we demean others we end up demeaning ourselves.

Making the Private Public

The ministry is full of boundaries we must not cross. We are invited into the most intimate and often painful moments of people's lives. We are with them in times of joy and times of crises. And these experiences make for very good stories and examples to help others who are going through the same joys and crises. The question becomes, when and what may we share? When are we allowed to make the private public?

Protect Your Family

Our respective children are now grown, but when they were young, they made for wonderful sermon stories and illustrations. The younger they were, the cuter their comments. Likewise, who doesn't like to complain about the things that teenagers do or don't do? We quickly learned that our children, especially as they got older, did not always appreciate being used as sermon fodder. And they really did not like to be surprised in the middle of the sermon. Our advice: no matter how good the story may seem to be, don't use it. Our children may love it when everyone comes to see them in the school play. But the day will come when they do not want that spotlight and it will arrive before you think it will. However, as Lucy learned, if she asked their permission and told them what she was going to share—letting them have veto power if they didn't want the story told—they came to enjoy their celebrity status. That is crucial.

Protect Your Parishioners

We must ask people if it is permissible to share their experiences in the pulpit. We need to ask permission to share the joys as well as to share the struggles. That means we need to be able to explain why we would like to make their private lives public. If we have received permission, their lives can serve as a witness of what God can and is doing to make the wounded whole. In the end, however, there are intimate details of their lives and our lives that we must never share. It also means that you can't decide on Saturday morning that someone's story is the perfect illustration. People need time to decide, and the fact that we have waited until the last moment should never be pressure for why someone needs to say *yes* now. When you ask permission to use someone's story, make sure that there is enough time for that person to debrief the wisdom of saying *yes* with other people in their closest circle of support.

Protect Yourself

Do not think that you can hide the details of someone's story by telling these stories when you move to a new congregation. Resist the temptation. Two reasons. First, someone in the new community will recognize who you are talking about. Second, if parishioners discover that you pass these stories on when you think no one will know, they might decide never to share their story with you. If your listeners begin to feel as though they may one day serve as sermon illustrations, in which you betray the confidence of intimate details of their lives, they will cease to share those details with you. Instead of being their pastor, you just come off as someone always on the prowl for good sermon illustrations. This means that even if you change enough of the details that no one will ever know who it was, people still make decisions about whether you are a person from whom they would seek spiritual counsel.

Once, while preaching a sermon in Washington, DC, Lucy told of an experience that she had over five years earlier in Iowa City. Lucy and her husband had been standing on a low pedestrian bridge that crossed over a river near the campus of the University of Iowa. As a group of students floated in the water beneath their feet, one of the young men was pulled under by the current. Although his friends tried to reach him, he drowned. Witnessing this tragedy of an untimely death made her acutely aware of Jesus' call to repent now, not later (Luke 13:5). When the service was over, one of the people leaving stopped to introduce himself as a visitor in the congregation that day.

What was startling and a bit eerie was the man told her he, too, had been on the bank of the river that day. He also watched the young man drown. We simply never know who will be there when we preach. So we need to preach as if the people who were part of whatever story we tell may be in our hearing that day. In an age in which many of our sermons are posted on the Internet, it is not as impossible as you may think.

Microwave Sermons

Perhaps one of the greatest missteps that today's busy, overworked, over-committed preachers make is that they do not devote enough time to the challenging and important task of preaching.

We live in an age during which we have come to believe that all things can and should be done instantly. Internet, texting, microwaves, and even international travel lull us into an instantaneous mentality. We get frustrated if our Internet is slow or if our text is not answered immediately.

But thoughtful, enriching, stimulating sermons are not produced on Saturday night. We cannot pop our text in an exegesis microwave and think that a sermon comparable to one with which we wrestled all week will come out. That is a recipe for dull sermons (see above). Remember, Jacob had to wrestle all night before he was blessed. We and our congregations will be blessed through our preaching if we are willing to put in the time, effort, and energy required. Harry Emerson Fosdick was said to devote one hour of work for every minute preached. Shrug that off as crazy, but remember that you had to arrive early at Fosdick's church if you wanted to actually hear rather than just read what he preached that morning.

So, one of the greatest challenges of preaching has nothing to do with biblical or theological scholarship. Rather, it is the challenge of carving out time for sermon preparation and holding hard and fast to that commitment. Faithful preaching demands that you make an appointment with yourself and then keep that appointment just as you do all of your other appointments. Unfortunately, so many crises present themselves throughout the day and the week, we all too willingly give up that sermon preparation time so that we can minister to the hurting people that present themselves.

Time management and time control become an important part of our preaching; tell people that we can see them—just not at 10 a.m. on Monday morning. What is crucial to remember is that you do not need to tell people why you cannot see them. You would not tell them the name of a person you might be meeting with; why would you tell them that is your sermon-preparation time?

Look at any list put forward by a congregation describing the qualities they are looking for in a pastor. In nine out of ten lists the number-one characteristic will be excellent preaching. However, the next question will be, is that congregation willing to afford their preacher the time that excellent preaching demands? Study, reading, reflection, writing, and rewriting are all part of responsible preaching. And they all take time. To be a responsible preacher is to be a devoted, timely preacher.

Forgive and Begin Again

Finally, we return to the unfortunate preacher at the outset of our abcederium of missteps, the one whose stomach dropped in the sermonic moment when she realized she had stepped over the line from responsible to irresponsible preaching. While she may have only committed a misdemeanor, she recognized that she had failed God and failed her listeners.

A crucial dimension of preaching is recognizing, confessing, repenting, and beginning again. We all make mistakes and missteps. It is important for preachers to forgive themselves and continue on. We are not perfect. We will never be perfect. And we preach always with that knowledge and with that forgiveness.

Over and over again in the Scriptures we read of those whom God called who protested that call. "Why would you call me," they ask. And they are not at a loss for reasons they should not preach: slow of tongue, too young, unqualified, and sinful. Nevertheless, God touches their tongues, ignores their lack of eloquence or youth, and bids them continue. We must do likewise.

FOR FURTHER READING

Harry Emerson Fosdick. "What Is the Matter with Preaching?" Reprinted in *What Is the Matter with Preaching Today?* Ed. Mike Graves. Louisville, KY: Westminister John Knox, 2004.

> The other essays in this same volume that explore and expand this same question for today are by David L. Bartlett, David Buttrick, Ernest T. Campbell, Fred B. Craddock, Marva Dawn, Anna Carter Florence, Mike Graves, Cleophus J. Larue, Thomas G. Long, Euguene L. Lowry, and Barbara Brown Taylor.

Lucy Lind Hogan. "The Virtuous Preacher: Even in 'Terrible, Horrible, No Good, Very Bad Weeks.'" Chapter 7 in *Graceful Speech: An Invitation to Preaching.* Louisville, KY: Westminster John Knox, 2006.

Becoming ☙ Responsible ❧ for the Faith We Proclaim

We have canvassed a variety of pulpit sins, pulpit missteps, and unthinking mistakes along the way. Our approach has identified six primary sins of pulpit practices that represent irresponsible preaching. Recall that beside the human dimensions of ethos, pathos, and logos, our approach is guided by the twin virtues of reliability and faithfulness we believe are at the heart of a virtue ethics of responsible preaching practice. As we invite you collectively to take seriously these virtues, consider two stories of preachers in the Bible—two Joppa stories.

A TALE OF TWO PREACHERS

The first of these Joppa stories presents the case of Jonah. When the word of the Lord comes to him, calling him to preach to the residents of Nineveh concerning their wickedness, Jonah heads for the seaport of Joppa instead and books passage on a ship bound for Tarshish (later known as Tarsus in southern Asia Minor). The last thing he wants to do is head east to obey God and preach to the Ninevites. (Nineveh was a city across the Tigris River from modern-day Mosul, Iraq.) When he finally preaches to these people and they do repent of their wickedness because of his preaching, he is disgusted. He complains to God that the reason he went down to Joppa to book passage west rather than head east was because he feared that these people might do exactly what they did: repent. He knew that, in his mercy, God might forgive them and deliver the city of Nineveh from judgment. "Just kill me now!" he sulks (Jonah 4:3)—anything but having to sit and watch the unrighteous be forgiven by the God of mercy. In a deeply ironic biblical tale, Jonah is depicted as a rebellious, irresponsible preacher who had no respect for the people to whom he was called to preach and had no desire to be faithful to the call to preach repentance to these Assyrian foreigners.

There are very few references to Joppa in the New Testament. The most prominent is also a story in which a character must choose to respond to God's call to preach good news. It's a story that presents us with the case of Peter praying to God on a rooftop.

In this story Peter is called by God to preach the good news to the household of Cornelius. Peter is in Joppa when the servants of the Roman centurion reach him. That day he had already experienced a rooftop vision from God that challenged the very essence of his ethnic presumption of Jewish racial privilege. But unlike Jonah, he accepts the counsel of God to preach the gospel before people he would formerly have believed to be unworthy of God's grace and mercy. And when he sees obvious evidence of the presence of the Holy Spirit as part of their response to what he preached, "he ordered them to be baptized in the name of Jesus Christ" (Acts 10:48).

When challenged by church leaders in Judea for breaking rank regarding this racial imperative, Peter recounted his experience of the vision given to him by God, the receptivity of his listeners, and the demonstration of the Spirit's power. "Who was I," he responded, "that I could hinder God?" This testimony resulted, Luke tells us, in the Judean Christian community praising God, saying, "Then God has given even to the Gentiles the repentance that leads to life" (Acts 11:17-18). In a story clearly told as a contrast to that of Jonah, Peter is presented as a preacher who transcends his cultural prejudices to accord deep respect to his listeners and true faithfulness in gospel proclamation.

The book of Jonah offers a story of irresponsible practice by a prophet who preaches in spite of his listeners and in spite of what God desired from him as faithfulness. The book of Acts offers a story of a prophetic preacher tearing down boundaries in an extraordinary act of cross-cultural respect for listeners and the pursuit of gospel faithfulness. Jonah is not redeemed at the close of his story and stands as an example of an irresponsible, unreliable preacher; Peter stands as his countertype—the prototypical responsible preacher.

We believe Luke has crafted this story of Peter as a reliable preacher with a view to provide readers with the appropriate means to think about the character qualities of reliability and faithfulness. In this tale of two preachers (with Joppa provided as a clue to ensure the connection is made), we discover that integrity with regard to the listeners and faithfulness to gospel purpose must matter in pulpit practice. These measures represent the Christian core of our proposal of an ethics of responsible pulpit practices.

Practicing Pulpit Virtues

Preachers are called to a vocation of *pistos*—to embody respect for listeners and faithfulness to gospel purposes in the preaching ministries. Preachers become responsible for the faith they proclaim through their intentionality in guarding their character and acting within the bounds of a credo they have adopted regarding pulpit practices. We believe these practices can be sustained through the choice to pursue authenticity, humility, carefulness, passion, courteousness, and being a "namer of God" in life's situations.

Character

When we adopt these capabilities as practices, as the habitual ways in which we choose to engage in the work of our calling, we are making character central to our moral compass in what it means to be people through whom a pulpit ministry becomes the means to express the deep love of Christ and to serve as one entrusted with a message of reconciliation that "in Christ God was reconciling the world to himself" (2 Cor. 5:19). Character matters. Character does not happen, however, simply because we are good people with good intentions. Character is refined by challenges. Our lives are invariably complex messy affairs in which we are always called to make choices, many of which are fine, acceptable, occasionally good enough, and sometimes very difficult.

We have all heard the maxim, "Character is in the choices you make when no one is looking." There is a measure of truth in that dictum, but we believe that character is better demonstrated in the choices we make when people are looking. In his profound declaration of freedom on the steps of the Lincoln Memorial, Martin Luther King Jr. said, "I have a dream that my four little children will one day live in a nation where they will not be judged by the color of their skin, but by the content of their character." The measure of our character is that we will be judged by others for how we have acted and for the choices we make that affect others. Character is the choice to practice virtues that call us to be the person we hope to be.[1]

Credo

When it comes to preaching we believe that unthinking mistakes can turn into pulpit missteps, which, if not brought to account by some commitment we have made to responsible conduct, can lead to irresponsible and sinful behavior in our pulpit practice. What is needed is a clear conception of virtuous pulpit practice that is capable of sustaining what we have called the *communio sanctorum*. We believe that such a claim on our ministry may best be served by devising a credo of responsible character in pulpit ministry.

A credo is a briefly stated summary of what a person believes in regard to some matter. In modern use, a credo is often composed with a specific view to morally appropriate conduct. It functions as an ethical declaration of intent. It is written by a person in order to guide that individual when faced with a moral challenge. Like a crisis plan in an organization, the credo is there to help a person make wise choices when faced with a dilemma or worse. The credo is there to remind that person of his or her vocational call to serve the high road of character rather than the detour of expediency.

If you have read this far you have a fair idea of what Lucy and Bob believe is important for preachers to consider when it comes to the character of their pulpit practice. This is where we invite you to take the next step. Take out your notebook and begin to draft what you believe. This is an invitation to devise your own credo of responsible pulpit practice with respect to your listeners and in faithfulness to gospel purposes in your preaching ministry. Make sure it is grounded in a deeply apprehended sense of self and your confessional identity and its traditions, in your vocational calling, and in what it means to you that first and foremost both you and your ministry to preach belong to God. Let the pulpit virtues we have raised up in this volume guide the way. Then add those we have missed that are especially relevant to you.

Professor Ronald J. Allen of Christian Theological Seminary composed a general "Code of Ethics" for preachers recently. We think it is a fine statement and have included it as an Appendix in this book. It's a great place to start your thinking for formulating your own credo.

THE GREATEST OF THESE . . .

Too many of us can imagine how uncomfortable Peter was as he stood on that early morning staring at the sand below his feet, unable to look into the face of the risen Christ. Only days before, in very different, very difficult circumstances, he had denied that he even knew his friend and teacher, not once, but three times. Now the one whom he had pledged to follow to the end had appeared before him, risen from the grave. Christ asked Peter a question three times, "Do you love me?" (John 21:15-17). Like Peter, we know that there have been times in our lives, in our preaching, when we denied Christ. We have not shown how much we love God or our neighbors. We, too, stare at our feet, tongue-tied.

We have explored some of the virtues that we believe help preachers loosen their tongues and become responsible and faithful to their calling. We also know that there are many more virtues that remain to be explored. But we believe that, in the end, there is one virtue that underlies all that we say and do.

When it came to the four cardinal virtues, there was the understanding that, "the virtue of prudence is the mold and 'mother' of all the other cardinal virtues, of justice, fortitude, and temperance."[2] Prudence, right thinking, common sense, they believed, made one ready to practice the other virtues. But we think that Paul challenges us to think, rather, that it is love that makes us ready to practice all other gifts, graces, and virtues:

I will show you a still more excellent way . . . (1 Cor. 12:31)

faith, hope and love abide, these three;
and the greatest of these is love. (1 Cor. 13:13)

We preach because God's love has filled us and called us. And out of that love we, in turn, preach of God's redeeming, life-giving love. We hope that, in some small way, we have helped you begin to reach down into that love to enrich and encourage you in your desire to become responsible for the faith we proclaim.

A Code of Ethics for Preachers

Ronald J. Allen is the Nettie Sweeney and Hugh Th. Miller Professor of Preaching and New Testament, Christian Theological Seminary

Source: Ronald J. Allen, "A Code of Ethics for Preachers," *Encounter* 66, no. 4 (Autumn 2005): 343-48. Reprinted by permission.

The following code of ethics for preachers is written in the form of promises that preachers can make to God, the congregation, themselves, and the world. Although the idea for such a code arose in the course of discussing the issues of preaching and plagiarism, this code goes beyond that immediate concern to cover a range of essential aspects of preaching. The code moves from items pertaining to broader life matters necessary for preaching, to the preparation and embodiment of the sermon itself, to reflection upon the sermon and learning from occasions of preaching.

1. I will regularly engage in the *practices* of my religious tradition so that I may be as faithful a representative of that tradition as possible.

2. Recognizing that my physical condition contributes to the attention and energy that I can give to sermon preparation, I will maintain a *lifestyle* of appropriate diet, exercise, and attention to psychological and interpersonal matters.

3. I will be aware of how preaching has been and is understood in the *denomination or movement* in whose name I am called to preach as well as in the broader tradition of which I am part, and I will maintain a vital, critical relationship with that tradition.

4. Each time I prepare a sermon, I will *pray* to be open to the movement of the Spirit.

5. Over the seasons of preaching, I will speak as much as I can of the *whole counsel of God* as is necessary for the growth of the congregation and my own growth in faith and witness and in faithfulness to the purposes of God as understood through Scripture, tradition, reason, and experience—affirming, challenging, questioning, weeping, laughing, and otherwise speaking, as needed.

6. I will remember that the sermon is a *part of the service of worship* and will try to shape the sermon so that it functions appropriately as a part of the service.

7. I will engage in *pastoral listening* to the congregation and its context (attending to all ethnicities, genders, ages, and other social locations in the community) as well as to the Bible and other resources that nurture the life of the congregation so that I may bring into optimum conversation the congregation's context and the resources that help us interpret the divine presence and leading.

8. I will take necessary steps to *prepare each sermon*, recognizing that in the moment of preaching, unanticipated insights may come to me that could affect the sermon.

9. I recognize that I may be called to preach at any moment, but *I will not intentionally be unprepared to preach.* If I am in a tradition that practices impromptu preaching, I will follow patterns of spirituality that help me always be ready to discern and respond to the leading of the Holy Spirit.

10. I will not repeat my own sermons from one time and place in another setting *without reconsidering themes that I may have used previously* in connection with the new occasion.

11. I will *set aside for sermon preparation the times* of the day and the week in which I am able to do my best work in putting together the sermon.

12. While I am called to listen to the Bible and others in helping the congregation identify the divine presence and purposes, *I will do my own work in sermon preparation* in conversation with interpretive helps and insights from others.

13. In the sermon, I will indicate *when I use material from others* that offers a distinctive idea, phrasing, story, anecdote, or other material. I will either directly cite the source or indirectly signal that the thought or phraseology comes from another person. The key phrase here is a distinctive, something good judgment recognizes as dissimilar from material found in other research resources.

14. I will honor *the integrity of others* with and of whom I speak in the sermon, such as the Bible, witnesses from tradition, and those to whom I turn in the course of preparing the sermon. I will make every effort not

to impose my own preferences for meaning upon them but will try to let them speak in their distinct voices.

15. I will *maintain my own integrity* in the message, saying what I truly believe and do not believe, and never misrepresent my own convictions.

16. I will *speak respectfully and fairly* of all whom I mention in the sermon. I will not speak derisively or cynically or make fun, but I will represent them clearly, honestly, with sensitivity, and in such ways that they would recognize themselves in the way that I speak about them.

17. I will *maintain confidentiality* in the pulpit with respect to those things that are told to me either explicitly or implicitly in confidence, including things told to me in confidence by church members, families, friends, and the wider community, both in my present congregation and in previous congregations.

18. If I refer during the sermon, either directly or indirectly, to members of the congregation or others who are known personally by the congregation in ways that the congregation could recognize, I will *acquire permission before doing so.*

19. I will refrain *from using material that is gratuitously shocking, sentimental,* or otherwise inappropriate.

20. I will seek to *respect the capacity of the congregation to reflect critically* on the subject and direction of the sermon and will *avoid using the sermon for manipulation.*

21. As the time for the sermon approaches, I will attempt to *arrange my life* with respect to eating habits, rest, and related matters so that I can step into the pulpit with optimum energy for the sermon.

22. In the moment of preaching, I will endeavor to be *fully present to the congregation* and to the purpose of the message.

23. Across the span of my ministry, I will seek *critical feedback* on my preaching from the congregation and from peers and teachers of preaching to help keep my practice of preaching at the highest possible communicative level.

24. I will regularly take advantage of *continuing learning opportunities* in preaching, theology, ethics, the arts, congregational studies, the various social and physical sciences, popular culture, and other matters that can help me gain insights into the lives of individuals, families, neighborhoods, cities, states, nations, and the world.

25. I will attempt to *live* from day to day in ways that are consistent with the content of my preaching.

26. While I will do my best to interpret life from the perspective of the Transcendent, I will *recognize my own finitude* and that of my theological tradition and will attempt to remain open in a critical way to the possibility of fresh insights.

27. I will remember that the *purpose of preaching* is not to feed my own ego or showcase my artistry but to help the congregation discern the divine presence and leading.

28. I will remember that *I preach for the glory of God* and the care of all people and elements within God's creation.

NOTES

1. Irresponsible Preaching

1. Joseph Jeter, "'The Strange Case of Dr. Jekyll and [Rev.] Hyde Jr.': Preaching and the Internet," *Encounter* 66, no. 4 (2005): 318.

2. In the classroom, homileticians typically want to help students learn how to preach prophetically, preach justice, preach inclusively, preach mercy, and so on. See André Resner, ed., *Just Preaching* (St. Louis: Chalice, 2002); Christine Smith, ed., *Preaching Justice: Ethnic and Cultural Perspectives* (Cleveland: United Church Press, 1998/Wipf & Stock, 2008); Kathy Black, *A Healing Homiletic: Preaching and Disability* (Nashville: Abingdon Press, 1996); etc. When homileticians write about ethics the focus tends to be about enabling *"preachers to contribute to the ethical formation and behavior of a people"* through preaching (e.g., Art Van Setters, *Preaching and Ethics* [St. Louis: Chalice Press, 2004], 2; italics his) or to explore a particular theoretical perspective as "An Ethic of . . ." preaching; e.g., Charles Campbell's *The Word before the Powers: An Ethic of Preaching* (Louisville: Westminster/John Knox, 2002): and John McClure, *Otherwise Preaching: A Postmodern Ethic for Homiletics* (St. Louis: Chalice, 2001).

3. Joe Trull and James Carter's *Ministerial Ethics: Moral Formation for Church Leaders*, 2nd ed. (Grand Rapids: Baker Academic, 2004) devotes only 3 pages out of 288 to dishonesty in preaching. Internet bloggers have given much more attention to this subject--especially the issue of plagiarism. The journal *Encounter* devoted six essays to the theme of "Preaching and Plagiarism" in 2005 (vol. 6.4). The essay, "A Code of Ethics for Preachers" by Ronald J. Allen, found in the appendix of this book, is taken from this collection of essays.

4. Exceptions are Ronald D. Sisk, *Preaching Ethically: Being True to the Gospel, Your Congregation, & Yourself* (Herndan, Va.: Alban Institute, 2008) and Raymond Bailey, "Ethics in Preaching," *Review and Expositor* 86 (1989): 533–46, anthologized in Michael Duduit, ed., *Handbook of Contemporary Preaching* (Nashville: Broadman Press, 1992), 549–61. A third book noted historically is Raymond W. McLaughlin, *The Ethics of Persuasive Preaching* (Grand Rapids: Baker Book House, 1979).

5. See Samuel Wells, *Transforming Fate into Destiny: The Theological Ethics of Stanley Hauerwas* (Eugene, Ore.: Cascade Books, 2004), 38. Much of the argument of this section has been shaped by Wells's reading of Hauerwas's theological ethics.

6. The four cardinal virtues—temperance, wisdom, justice, and courage—were actually formulated first by Plato ("No other part of virtue is like knowledge, or like justice, or like courage, or like temperance, or like holiness?" *Protagoras* 330b) and adapted by church fathers Ambrose and Augustine as the cardinal virtues for Christian piety. In place of Plato's "holiness" they added the Christian virtues that come from God: faith, hope, and love. Another list, the Seven Heavenly Virtues, was devised by church leaders as a set of virtuous Christian practices meant to challenge each of the temptations of the seven deadly sins: chastity~lust, temperance~gluttony, charity~greed, diligence~sloth, patience~wrath, kindness~envy, and humility~pride.

7. As cited in Linda L. Belleville, *2 Corinthians* (Downers Grove, Ill.: IVP Academic, 1996), 165.

8. For example, the *Listening to Listeners* Lilly Endowment foundation study examines the character of the preacher first in its list of criteria. There is a reason. Aristotle once argued that, of the three primary resources of strategic reasoning, "Character is almost, so to speak, the most authoritative form of persuasion." John S. McClure, Ronald J. Allen, Dale P. Andrews, L. Susan Bon, Dan P. Mosely, and G. Lee Ramsey Jr., *Listening to Listeners: Homiletical Case Studies* (St. Louis: Chalice Press, 2004); Ronald J. Allen, *Hearing the Sermon: Relationship/Content/Feeling* (St. Louis: Chalice Press, 2004). For the citation from Aristotle, see *On Rhetoric: A Theory of Civic Discourse*, 2nd ed., George A. Kennedy, trans. (New York: Oxford University Press, 2007), 39 [I.2.4].

9. William O. Avery and A. Roger Gobbel, "The Word of God and the Words of the Preacher,"

in *A Reader on Preaching: Making Connections,* ed. David Day, Jeff Astley, and Leslie Francis (Burlington, Vt.: Ashgate, 2005), 266–75. Originally published in *Review of Religious Research* 22, no. 5 (1980): 41–53.

10. For example, one study that surveyed more than 15,000 global leaders and managers, employed 400 specific case studies, and interviewed 40 respected organizational leaders, concluded that personal credibility is the one quality that best describes those individuals whom people trust when choosing to follow a leader. James M. Kouzes and Barry Z. Posner, *Credibility: How Leaders Gain and Lose It, and Why People Demand It* (San Francisco: Jossey-Bass, 1993).

11. Aristotle, *Rhetetoric* I.2.1, 1355b.

12. See the discussion of Aristotle's *Rhetoric* at the online *Stanford Encyclopedia of Philosophy* at http://plato.stanford.edu/entries/aristotle-rhetoric/#4.1.

13. See David S. Cunningham, *Faithful Persuasion: In Aid of a Rhetoric of Christian Theology* (Notre Dame: University of Notre Dame Press, 1991).

14. Wayne Booth, *The Rhetoric of Rhetoric: The Quest for Effective Communication* (Malden, Mass.: Wiley-Blackwell, 2004), 54. We raise Booth's work here to help readers see how a contemporary philosopher of communication looks to the resources of the rhetorical tradition to arrive at a secular ethics of responsible communicative practice. Where we choose to work the ethics of *ethos, pathos,* and *logos,* Booth proposes a contemporary ethics of rhetoric by taking up Aristotle's original notion of speech situations (e.g., judicial, deliberative, and epideictic) and translating them into educational, political, and mass media locations today.

15. Wayne Booth, *The Company We Keep: An Ethics of Fiction* (Berkeley: University of California Press, 1988).

16. This understanding of preaching's purpose used throughout this book is taken from Robert Stephen Reid, *The Four Voices of Preaching* (Grand Rapids: Brazos Press, 2006), 220–21.

17. Aristotle, *Rhetoric,* 2.2.5-6 (1378a); see George Kennedy, *Aristotle on Rhetoric: A Theory of Civic Discourse,* 2nd ed. (New York: Oxford University Press, 2007), 112.

18. The biographical film *The King's Speech* was directed by Tom Hooper and was released in December 2010.

19. This is from Martin Heidegger's *Being and Time (1962:178)* as cited by George Kennedy, in *Aristotle on Rhetoric,* 115.

20. In a rather direct fashion, Aristotle wrote that affective efforts to influence occur by way of "arguments [*logoi*] when we show the truth or the apparent truth from whatever is persuasive in each case"; Aristotle, *Rhetoric,* 1.2.6 (1356a); see Kennedy, *Aristotle on Rhetoric,* 39.

2. The Pretender

1. The interview aired on *The Tavis Smiley Show* on Wednesday, April 10, 2002. Retrieved in 2002 at http://www.npr.org/ramfiles/tavis/20020410.tavis.01.ram.

2. Comment by Richard Lischer on *The Tavis Smiley Show.*

3. Comment by Noel Jones on *The Tavis Smiley Show.*

4. Tim Keller in "Five Leaders Examine Plagiarism in Preaching," retrieved at The Gospel Coalition National Conference, April 12-14, 2010. Retrieved at http://www.sermoncentral.com/articlec.asp?article=five-leaders-examine-plagiarism-in-preaching&ac=true.

5. See Carter Shelly, "Preaching and Plagiarism: A Guide for Introduction to Preaching Students," *Homiletic* 27, no. 2 (2002): 9; Shelly notes that he returned to a congregation that had been reduced by a third because of the debate.

6. Craig Larson of *Preaching Today* gives instructions on how to do this with integrity at http://pttranscripts.stores.yahoo.net/usotpesewiin.html. The fact that explanations for how to do it with integrity are being offered indicates that the practice is sufficiently widespread to need this kind of advice. See the discussion of this in Joseph R. Jeter Jr., "'The Strange Case of Dr. Jekyll and [Rev.] Hyde Jr.': Preaching and the Internet," *Encounter* 66, no. 4 (Autumn 2005): 317–22.

7. Michael Luo, "Pastor Who Plagiarized Finds a Church Willing to Forgive," *The New York Times,* July 28, 2006, A 25.

8. Rick Warren, "Purpose-Driven Preaching: An Interview with Rick Warren," interview by Michael Dudit. Retrieved at http://www.preaching.com/sermons/11565775/page-14/. In context Warren's primary point appears to be that preachers should feel free to use his material without worrying about attribution.

9. Thomas G. Long, "Stolen Goods: Tempted to Plagiarize," *Christian Century* (April 17, 2007): 19–20. The open source versus plagiarism debate is larger than its application here to preaching. The argument we develop here might not apply to other mediums in which the issue of the authenticity of personal testimony is not at issue.

10. Randy Cohen, "Divine Cheat," *The New York Times Magazine* (October 13, 2002), retrieved at http://www.nytimes.com/2002/10/13/magazine/the-way-we-live-now-10-13-02-the-ethicist-divine-cheat.html?scp=1&sq=The+Ethicist++Divine+Cheat&st=nyt&pagewanted=print.

11. This is Rick Lischer's argument as reported in Dean Smith, "An Era When the Art of the Sermon Has Declined," *The New York Times*, March 30, 2002, late edition, sec. B.

12. This solution (distinguishing between contribution and attribution) belongs to Michael Graves, "Preaching and Plagiarizing," *Clergy Journal* (2004): 18–19, and revised for publication in "Attribution and Contribution: Two Ways to Avoid Plagiarism in Preaching," *Encounter* 66, no. 4 (2005): 323–30.

13. John Indermark, "Ethics and the Use of Sermon Resources: Shifting Lines in Plagiarism and Preaching," *Clergy Journal* (October 2007): 29–30.

14. Jamie Buckingham, "Pulpit Plagiarism," in *Leadership Handbook of Preaching and Worship*, ed. James D. Berkley (Grand Rapids: Baker Books, 1992).

15. Shelly, "Preaching and Plagiarism," 9.

16. Ibid., 10.

17. Steve Sjogren, "Don't Be Original—Be Effective!" *Rick Warren's Ministry Toolbox 250* (March 15, 2006). Available at http://www.pastors.com/blogs/ministrytoolbox/archive/2006/03/13/Don_1920_t-be-original-_1320_-be-effective_2100_.aspx.

18. Augustine, *On Christian Doctrine*, IV.29.

19. Karl Barth, *Homiletics*, trans. Geoffrey W. Bromily and Donald E. Daniels (Louisville: Westminster John Knox Press, 1991), 82–83. It should be noted that Barth believed so strongly that the sermon should be the witness of the preacher that he had little patience for including anything in the sermon that might need attribution.

20. We are aware that these writers might not make such claims, but they serve as useful affirmations for thinking our way through the issue of creativity at this point.

21. Long, "Stolen Goods," 21.

22. Ed Stetzer, "Preaching, Plagiarism, and Sermon Central." Available at http://www.edstetzer.com/2008/05/preaching_plagiarism_and_sermo_1.html.

3. The Egoist

1. Skip Hollandsworth, "The Private Hell of Joel Gregory," *Texas Monthly Magazine* 22, no. 10 (October 1994): 140–42.

2. Joel Gregory, *Too Great a Temptation: The Seductive Power of America's Super Church* (Fort Worth: Summit Group, 1994). In an essay about W. A. Criswell as a theologian in the Baptist tradition, Southeast Baptist Theological Seminary president, Paige Patterson, finds Gregory's book "sometimes accurate but almost wholly false" (391n9). He clearly treats Gregory's account as self-serving but still agrees that the book speaks substantively to the issue of ego and calling; see Paige Patterson, "W. A. Criswell," in *Theologians of the Baptist Tradition*, ed. Timothy George and David S. Dockery (Nashville: Broadman, 2001), 237. Others have accepted Gregory's story as deeply revealing of the problem of "unguarded ego" and ministry; for example, see the adaptation of this story by playwright David Rambo, *God's Man in Texas*.

3. The phrase "in the shadow of the unguarded ego" is from the liner notes of *Greg Warner, Executive Editor of Associated Baptist Press*, found on the back cover of *Too Great a Temptation*.

4. Gregory, *Too Great a Temptation*, 8.

5. Ibid., 18.

6. Ibid., 319.

7. On a trinitarian perspective in preaching, see Lucy Hogan, *Graceful Speech: An Invitation to Preaching* (Louisville: Westminster John Knox, 2006), 3–14.

8. We draw this phrase "cross-purposes" from André Resner, *Preacher and Cross: Person and Message in Theology and Rhetoric* (Grand Rapids: Eerdmans, 1999), 106–18, and Resner, "At Cross Purposes: Gospel, Scripture and Experience in Preaching," in *Preaching Autobiography: Connecting the World of the Preacher and the World of the Text*, ed. David Fleer and Dave Bland (Abilene, Tex.: ACU Press, 2001), 64.

9. Donald Macleod, *The Problem of Preaching* (Philadelphia: Fortress Press, 1989), 41.

10. Phillips Brooks, *Lectures on Preaching* (New York: E. P. Dutton, 1877), 5.

11. In Richard Lischer, ed. *The Company of Preachers: Wisdom on Preaching* (Grand Rapids: Eerdmans, 2002), 58.

12. See André Resner, "Preacher as God's Mystery Steward," in *Slow of Speech and Unclean Lips: Contemporary Images of Preaching Identity*, ed. Robert Stephen Reid (Eugene, Ore.: Cascade, 2010), 71.

13. Christopher Lasch, *The Culture of Narcissism: American Life in an Age of Diminishing Expectations* (New York: Warner, 1979), 101.

14. Sandy Hotchkiss, *Why Is It Always About You? Saving Yourself from the Narcissists in Your Life* (New York: Free Press, 2002).

15. See the *Diagnostic and Statistical Manual of Mental Disorders*, 4th edition (1994), of the American Psychiatric Association, commonly referred to as DSM-IV. The American Psychiatric Association has determined that as many as one out of every one hundred people may meet the full criteria of these seven dimensions. See Hotchkiss, *Why Is It Always About You?* 30.

16. Resner, "At Cross Purposes," 64.

17. See Richard Thulin, *The "I" of the Sermon: Autobiography in the Sermon* (Minneapolis: Fortress Press, 1989).

18. See Fleer, *Preaching Autobiography*, 41–42.

19. Cited by William H. Willimon, "Foreword," in *Preaching Autobiography*, 13.

20. John Calvin, *Golden Booklet of the True Christian Life*, in *Devotional Classics: Selected Readings for Individuals and Groups*, ed. Richard J. Foster and James Bryan Smith (San Francisco: HarperOne, 1993), 137.

21. Richard J. Foster, *Prayer: Finding the Heart's True Home* (San Francisco: HarperSanFrancisco, 1992), 61

22. Augustine reminds us that "humility is the foundation of all the other virtues hence, in the soul in which this virtue does not exist there cannot be any other virtue except in mere appearance" (en.wikiquote.org/wiki/Augustine_of_Hippo).

23. Aurthur F. Holmes, "The Closing of the American Mind and the Opening of the Christian Mind," in *Faithful Learning and the Christian Scholarly Vocation*, ed. Douglas V. Henry and Bob R. Agee (Grand Rapids: Eerdmans, 2003), 103.

24. This is a summary of the substance rather than an actual verbatim quote of what John Claypool said.

25. Resner, "At Cross Purposes," 48–49.

26. Willimon, "Foreword," *Preaching Autobiography*, 13.

4. *The Manipulator*

1. Jimmy Swaggart, "I Have Sinned," February 21, 1988. You may watch portions of the sermon on several websites such as at http://abcnews.go.com/US/video/jimmy-swaggart-affair-apology-9876022 and http://www.americanrhetoric.com/speeches/jswaggartapologysermon.html.

2. Ibid.

3. Quentin Schultz, *Televangelism and American Culture: The Business of Popular Religion* (Grand Rapids: Baker, 1991), 104.

4. Giuliano successfully makes this case. Swaggart's "The Prize of the High Calling" sermon can be found in Michael J. Giuliano, *Thrice Born: The Rhetorical Comeback of Jimmy Swaggart* (Macon, Ga.: Mercer Press, 1999).

5. See "Glurge," Snopes.com at http://www.snopes.com/glurge/glurge.asp

6. Aristotle, *Rhetoric* 1404a.

7. Nathaniel Hawthorne, *The Scarlet Letter* (New York: Modern Library, 2000); all quotations from this edition can be found on pages 128–31.

8. Cited as a frontispiece for part 1 in Barbara Brown Taylor, *Leaving Church: A Memoir of Faith* (San Francisco: HarperOne, 2007), 1.

9. If a preacher is fabricating "true" stories to illustrate matters, see the issues of authenticity raised in chapter 2.

10. Quintilian, *Institutio Oratoria*, VI.2.7.

11. See Susan Forward, *Emotional Blackmail: When the People in Your Life Use Fear, Obligation, and Guilt to Manipulate You* (New York: HarperCollins, 1998).

12. G. Lee Ramsey Jr., *Care-full Preaching: From Sermon to Caring Community* (St. Louis: Chalice Press, 2000), 86.

13. Ibid.

14. Ibid., 86. Ramsey draws on distinctions made by Robert Wuthnow, "Religious Discourse as Public Rhetoric," *Communication Research* 15, no. 3 (June 1988): 332–33.

15. Ramsey, *Care-full Preaching*, 42.

16. Ibid., 39.

17. Ibid., 135.

18. Ibid.

19. Ibid., 138.

20. Ibid., 144.

21. Ibid., 143.

22. Though preaching is generally monological, many contemporary models of preaching explore ways to help preachers imagine ways to ensure that a variety of voices influence a final, dialogical shape of a sermon.

23. Mark Galli, "John Stott and the Weary Evangelical: What the Movement Looks Like at Its Best," *Christianity Today* at http://www.christianitytoday.com/ct/2011/augustweb-only/johnstottwearyevangelical.html.

24. This is our summary of key ideas in Galli's presentation of Stott's model.

5. *The Panderer*

1. Richard L. Berke, "The 1992 Campaign: Democrats Saying Clinton Is Cynical, Tsongas Goes on the Attack," *New York Times*, March 7, 1992, retrieved at http://www.nytimes.com/1992/03/07/us/the-1992-campaign-democrats-saying-clinton-is-cynical-tsongas-goes-on-the-attack.html.

2. Paul Simon, *Our Culture of Pandering* (Carbondale: Southern Illinois University Press, 2003), xi.

3. Jennifer L. Lord, *Finding Language and Imagery: Words for Holy Speech* (Minneapolis: Fortress Press, 2010), 11–12.

4. See further in Lucy Lind Hogan, *Graceful Speech: An Invitation to Preaching* (Louisville: Westminster John Knox, 2006), 59–60.

5. Marsha G. Witten, *All Is Forgiven: The Secular Message in American Protestantism* (Princeton, N.J.: Princeton University Press, 1993), 140. The nuances of theology can be lost in Witten's assumptions that the purpose of preaching is to present theology proper, but her critique is still quite important.

6. Neil Postman, *Amusing Ourselves to Death: Public Discourse in the Age of Show Business* (New York: Penguin Books, 1985), 13.

7. Ibid., 116–17.

8. Neil Postman, "The New Technologies and the Human Person: Communicating the Faith in the New Millennium," March 27, 1998, retrieved at http://www.mat.upm.es/~jcm/neil-postman—five-things.html. We encourage readers to search out and read the arguments supporting each claim.

9. M. Rex Miller, *The Millennium Matrix: Reclaiming the Past, Reframing the Future of the Church* (San Francisco: Jossey-Bass, 2004), 45.

10. David J. Randolph, *The Renewal of Preaching in the Twenty-First Century: The Next Homiletics* (Eugene, Ore.: Cascade, 2009), xi.

11. Postman, *Amusing Ourselves*, 98.

12. Senator Chuck Grassley (office of), "Grassley Seeks Information from Six Media-based Ministries," November 6, 2007, retrieved at http://grassley.senate.gov/news/Article.cfm?customel_dataPageID_1502=12011.

13. Senator Chuck Grassley (office of), "Grassley Releases Review of Tax Issues Raised by Media-based Ministries," January 6, 2011, retrieved at http://grassley.senate.gov/news/Article.cfm?customel_dataPageID_1502=30359.

14. Jesse James DeConto, "Camp Meeting," *The Christian Century*, August 9, 2011, 13.

15. Ibid.

16. Len Wilson and Jason Moore, *Digital Storytellers: The Art of Communicating the Gospel in Worship* (Nashville: Abingdon Press, 2002), 75–76. Wilson notes that "sermon-centered worship, if based on the Bible at all, is mostly the presentation of one person's understanding of biblical stories; based on his or her private, quiet analysis of biblical texts" (77). There is an important question facing the pulpit as we enter the digital age: how to communicate to the whole person and the role that story and image play in this task.

17. Rex Miller's *Millenium Matrix* is a provocative introductory guide to grasping the significant ways in which individuals who embody the digital cultural consciousness are remarkably different in how their faith orientation compares to individuals whose faith consciousness has largely been structured by the broadcast-era, the print-era, or the oral-era ways of knowing.

18. William H. Willimon, *Pastor: The Theology and Practice of Ordained Ministry* (Nashville: Abingdon Press, 2002), 95–96.

19. Rachel Mikva, ed. *Broken Tablets* (Woodstock, Vt.: Jewish Lights, 1999), 38

20. Carl S. Dudley and Dale A. Roozen, *A Report on Religion in the United States Today* (Hartford Institute for Religion Research, 2003), 2.

21. Simon, *Our Culture of Pandering*, 118.

22. Ibid., 100.

23. Ibid., 123.

24. Ibid., 123–25.

25. Jeffrey L. Sheler, "Spiritual America: This Nation 'Under God' Is Deeply Conflicted over the Role of Religion in Society," *U.S. News and World Report*, March 27, 1994, retrieved at http://www.usnews.com/usnews/culture/articles/940404/archive_012680_6.htm.

26. Clark M. Williamson and Ronald J. Allen, *The Teaching Minister* (Louisville: Westminster John Knox Press, 1991), 70.

27. Ibid., 85.

28. Ibid., 87–93.

29. James F. Kay, *Preaching and Theology* (St. Louis: Chalice Press, 2007), vii.

30. Stephen King, "Afterword," in *Full Dark, No Stars* (New York: Scribner, 2010), 365.

6. *The Demagogue*

1. Alan Brinkley, *Voices of Protest, Huey Long, Father Coughlin and the Great Depression* (New York: Knopf, 1982), 83.

2. Larry Witham, *A City Upon a Hill: How Sermons Changed the Course of American History* (New York: HarperOne, 2007), 230.

3. T. H. Watkins, *The Hungry Years: A Narrative History of the Great Depression in America* (New York: Henry Holt, 1995), 255.

4. Cited in James Shelton, "The Coughlin Movement and The New Deal," *Political Science Quarterly* 73, no. 3 (1958): 371.

5. See Michael Casey and Aimee Rowe, "'Driving Out the Money Changers': Radio Priest Charles E. Coughlin's Rhetorical Vision," *The Journal of Communication and Religion* 19, no. 1 (1996): 37–47.

6. Cited by Casey and Rowe, "The Coughlin Movement," from Daniel Berrigan, *To Dwell in Peace: An Autobiography* (San Francisco: Harper and Row, 1987), 67–68.

7. His popularity grew as he gave public voice to the fear Americans felt about how to wage a cold war of ideas rather than a hot war with soldiers on a battlefield. Because of his position of power, McCarthy could simply wave papers before witnesses as if they were accepted evidence of that person's collusion in communist activities.

8. Patricia Roberts-Miller, "Democracy, Demagoguery, and Critical Rhetoric," *Rhetoric and Public Affairs* 8 (2005): 462. Of course, the demagogue never suggests that she or he is scapegoating the out-group members; rather, they are justly being removed from exercising power or influence.

9. Erich Fromm, *Escape from Freedom* (New York: Rinehart, 1941), 36–37. Fromm maintained that people seek to avoid the responsibilities of freedom through three common escape mechanisms: accepting automaton conformity, accepting authoritarianism, or embracing destructiveness. We take up automaton conformity, he alleged, by yielding to group pressure to overcome uncertainty by being or acting in some preferred way. We escape responsibility, he believed, if we surrender control of our freedom to someone or thing that authoritatively promises to restore stability and safety in our lives. We embrace destructiveness, he concluded, when we scapegoat others to save ourselves from social forces that seem oppressive or make us feel helpless.

10. J. Justin Gustainis, "Demagoguery and Political Rhetoric: A Review of the Literature," *Rhetoric Society Quarterly* 20 (1990): 155, 158–60.

11. See MSNBC News David Shuster segment, "People for the American Way's Kathryn Kolbert on Rick Warren," retrieved at http://www.youtube.com/watch?v=AvuibnldEGk. For Kolbert's comments, see "Democratic Underground," December 19, 2008, retrieved at http://www.democraticunderground.com/discuss/duboard.php?az=view_all&address=132x8009565.

12. Reinhold Niebuhr, *The Nature and Destiny of Man* (New York: Charles Scribner's Sons, 1949), 2:219–20.

13. Timothy Keller, *Counterfeit Gods: The Empty Promises of Money, Sex, and Power and the Only Hope That Matters* (New York: Dutton, 2009), 106–7.

14. A number of these principles as they relate to dogmatism in communication have been derived from Milton Rokeach, *The Open and Closed Mind: Investigations into the Nature of Belief Systems and Personality Systems* (New York: Basic Books, 1960).

15. As cited in Brad Hirschfield, *You Don't Have to Be Wrong for Me to Be Right: Finding Faith without Fanaticism* (New York: Harmony/Crown Publishing, 2007), 16–17.

16. Herbert W. Simons, *Persuasion in Society* (Thousand Oaks, Calif.: Sage Publications, 2001), 6–8.

17. *The Book of the Courtier* provides a definitive account of Renaissance court life. Kenneth Burke turns to this highly influential book because he is more interested in the rhetoric of wooing than winning. He believes it is the primary task of a communicator to establish rapport by way of identification with the audience (*A Rhetoric of Motives*, 46). On his exploration of courting and *The Book of the Courtier*, see Kenneth Burke, *A Rhetoric of Motives* (New York: Prentice-Hall, 1950), 221–33.

18. Baldassare Castiglione, *The Book of the Courtier* (1528), 1.26.

19. Eric Fromm, *The Sane Society* (New York: Holt, Rinehart, and Winston, 1955).

20. Hirschfield, *You Don't Have to Be Wrong*, 17–18.

7. *The Despot*

1. George Regas, "Interpreting Christ in a Pluralistic World." Washington National Cathedral, April 24, 2005, http://www.nationalcathedral.org/worship/sermonTexts/gfr050424.shtml.

2. Ibid.

3. Ibid.

4. Ibid.

5. Michael Maccomby, "Narcissistic Leaders: The Incredible Pros and Inevitable Cons," *Harvard Business Review* (January/February 2000): 70.

6. Ibid.

7. Barbara Brown Taylor, *Leaving Church: A Memoir of Faith* (San Francisco: HarperOne, 2007), 95. Effectiveness is an unacceptable goal for pastoral ministry. There are clergy whose primary strengths are care and nurture who also need to pay more attention to the need for organizational effectiveness. But success should never be a primary or first concern of faithful leadership of a congregation. What is needed is faithfulness to a gospel calling.

8. Eric W. Gritsch, *Toxic Spirituality: Four Enduring Temptations of Christian Faith* (Minneapolis: Fortress Press, 2009).

9. For a book-length exploration of the political despot and despotism, see Tom Ambrose, *The Nature of Despotism: From Caligula to Mugabe, the Making of Tyrants* (London: New Holland, 2008).

10. It is significant that 138 Muslim scholars and religious leaders have grounded their case for seeking peace between Christians and Muslims in Jesus' summary of Judaism's greatest commandment in "A Common Word Between Us and You," an open letter published in the *New York Times*, October 13, 2007. This letter and theological reflection on it by both Christian and Muslim theologians and political leaders can be found in Miroslav Volf, Ghazi bin Muhammad, and Melissa Yarrington, *A Common Word: Muslims and Christians on Loving God and Neighbor* (Grand Rapids: Eerdmans, 2010).

11. Charles Kimball, *When Religion Becomes Evil: Five Warning Signs* (New York: HarperOne, 2008), 47.

12. Paul Hill, "Why Shoot an Abortionist," retrieved at http://www.armyofgod.com/PHillonepage.html.

13. See Kimball, *When Religion Becomes Evil*, 52–53.

14. See Jessica Stern, *Terror in the Name of God: Why Religious Militants Kill* (New York: Ecco, 2003), xxvi.

15. Mashall Applewhite, "Planet Earth about to Be Recycled." This presentation can be viewed at http://www.youtube.com/watch?v=BDa2rwwZHeE.

16. Stern, *Terror in the Name of God*, 236. Declaring holy war is not the same thing as theological consideration of whether a particular war can be termed a "just war"; see Kimball, *When Religion Becomes Evil*, 178–82.

17. ABC News, "President Obama Says Terry Jones' Plan to Burn Korans Is 'A Destructive Act,'" retrieved at http://abcnews.go.com/GMA/president-obama-terry-jones-koran-burning-plan-destructive/story?id=11589122.

18. International News Website, "September 11 proposed as the International Day to Burn the Koran," retrieved at http://www.pleasingnews.com/tag/terry-jones/.

19. McClatchy News Service, "Fred Phelps' Daughter: 'Westboro Church Has Already Burned Qurans,'" retrieved at http://www.mcclatchydc.com/2010/09/09/100291/fred-phelps-daughter-westboro.html.

20. This is a phrase made famous by master rhetorician Kenneth Burke in defining a tendency in what it means to be human; Kenneth Burke, *Language as Symbolic Action* (Berkeley: University of California Press, 1966), 16.

21. Kimball, *When Religion Becomes Evil*, 7.

22. Abraham Heschel, *Man Is Not Alone: A Philosophy of Religion* (New York: Farrar, Straus and Giroux, 1976), 4. Heschel's thought is expressed, like that of Martin Buber before him, in an approach to understanding language as an event of meaning-making; it participates in the tradition of European philosophical hermeneutics and theology.

23. Heschel, *Man Is Not Alone*, 4–5.

24. See Robert Stephen Reid, "Preacher as One Entrusted," in *Slow of Speech and Unclean Lips: Contemporary Images of Preaching Identity*, ed. R. S. Reid (Eugene, Ore.: Cascade Books, 2010), 154–78.

25. Heschel, *Man Is Not Alone*, 8. Heschel intends for this claim to set up the exploration of his subject matter, but it serves equally well as an affirmation of the wonder with which all who preach should approach their task.

26. Ibid., 109; includes the previous quotation.

27. On this understanding of preaching, see Robert Stephen Reid, *The Four Voices of Preaching* (Grand Rapids: Brazos Press, 2006), 21–22.

28. Mary Catherine Hilkert, *Naming Grace: Preaching and the Sacramental Imagination* (New York: Continuum, 2000), 49–53.

29. André LaCocque and Paul Ricoeur, *Thinking Biblically: Exegetical and Hermeneutical Studies*, trans. David Pellauer (Chicago: University of Chicago Press, 1998), xii.

30. Stern, *Terror in the Name of God*, 296.

31. Miroslav Volf, *The End of Memory: Remembering Rightly in a Violent World* (Grand Rapids: Eerdmans, 2006), 127.

32. Ibid., 179–80.

8. Wait! Wait! There's More!

1. Harry Emerson Fosdick, "What Is the Matter with Preaching?" reprinted in *What Is the Matter with Preaching Today?* ed. Mike Graves (Louisville: Westminster John Knox, 2004), 9–10.

2. Ibid., 11.

Epilogue: Becoming Responsible for the Faith We Proclaim

1. For a marvelous collection of statements about character, see those collected by the folk at the Josephson Institute at http://josephsoninstitute.org/quotes/quotations.php?q=Character.

2. Josef Pieper, *The Four Cardinal Virtues* (Notre Dame: University of Notre Dame Press, 1966), 3.